26 February 2017

For Canon

with real joy for our
partnership in the Gospel

through

the Anglican Communion

Many blessings,

Ashley
†

"In light of the current crises of the Anglican Communion, this study of the origins of Reformation Anglicanism is particularly timely. The authors remind us why the Church of England adopted the confessional formularies that have characterized it since the sixteenth century and examine the relevance of these to the modern situation at home and abroad. Everyone with an interest in Anglicanism will benefit from looking afresh at its core principles, and the authors of this volume have done their best to demonstrate how those principles are still meaningful and relevant today."

Gerald Bray, Research Professor of Divinity, History, and Doctrine, Beeson Divinity School; author, *God Is Love* and *God Has Spoken*

"This book sketches some of the complex history of the Church of England from early beginnings to the shape of the present worldwide denomination, now about eighty million strong. More importantly, it calls contemporary Anglicans, often awash in doctrinal and moral confusion, to return to the primary sources and evangelical and Reformed doctrines of the English Reformation, if that Reformation is to fulfill its promise."

D. A. Carson, Research Professor of New Testament, Trinity Evangelical Divinity School; Cofounder, The Gospel Coalition

"This wonderful book reminds me of what the former archbishop of Canterbury Michael Ramsey said: 'To belittle the witness of the Reformers is to miss something of the meaning of the church of God.' I am so grateful to the authors for producing this book, which will help us to know what it means to be a church of God."

Mouneer Hanna Anis, Anglican Primate of Jerusalem and the Middle East; Chairman, The Anglican Global South

"This is a work that will serve contemporary Anglicanism permanently in helping readers understand that Reformation Anglicanism is simply biblical Christianity. In a time when many churches are doctrinally confused or morally compromised, readers will be encouraged to hold fast to the gospel and to fight against false teaching. I commend this book most highly and look forward to subsequent volumes in the library."

Nicholas D. Okoh, Anglican Primate of All Nigeria; Chairman, The Global Anglican Future Conference

Reformation Anglicanism

THE REFORMATION ANGLICANISM ESSENTIAL LIBRARY

VOLUME 1

REFORMATION ANGLICANISM

A Vision for Today's Global Communion

EDITED BY ASHLEY NULL
AND JOHN W. YATES III

WHEATON, ILLINOIS

Reformation Anglicanism: A Vision for Today's Global Communion

Copyright © 2017 by John Ashley Null and John W. Yates III

Published by Crossway
   1300 Crescent Street
   Wheaton, Illinois 60187

Cover design: Samuel Miller

First printing 2017

Printed in the United States of America

Hardcover ISBN: 978-1-4335-5213-7
ePub ISBN: 978-1-4335-5216-8
PDF ISBN: 978-1-4335-5214-4
Mobipocket ISBN: 978-1-4335-5215-1

Library of Congress Cataloging-in-Publication Data

Names: Null, Ashley, author, editor. | Yates, John W., 1974– author, editor.
Title: Reformation Anglicanism : a vision for today's global communion / edited by Ashley Null and John W. Yates III.
Description: Wheaton, Illinois : Crossway, 2017. | Series: The Reformation Anglicanism essential library ; volume 1 | Includes bibliographical references and index.
Identifiers: LCCN 2016026235 (print) | LCCN 2016030303 (ebook) | ISBN 9781433552137 (hc) | ISBN 9781433552144 (pdf) | ISBN 9781433552151 (mobi) | ISBN 9781433552168 (epub)
Subjects: LCSH: Anglican Communion—Doctrines. | Anglican Communion—History. | Church of England—Doctrines. | Church of England—History.
Classification: LCC BX5005 .R44 2017 (print) | LCC BX5005 (ebook) | DDC 283—dc23
LC record available at https://lccn.loc.gov/2016026235

Crossway is a publishing ministry of Good News Publishers.

TS		27	26	25	24	23	22	21	20	19	18	17
15	14	13	12	11	10	9	8	7	6	5	4	3	2	1

With loving gratitude
for the living legacy of
John Stott and J. I. Packer

Contents

Preface

Around the world today more than 80 million people in 165 countries identify themselves as Anglican Christians. The nature of that shared identity, however, is a subject of earnest discussion and often vigorous debate. Recent fissures within the Anglican Communion have left those who are part of it asking questions of foundational import: What does it mean to be Anglican? What is the nature of our global communion? To what extent are we bound to one another by shared doctrine, history, and culture? These critical questions lead to even deeper questions: What is the gospel? What is the nature of God's grace, our faith, and eternal life? What authority does Scripture possess, and how are we to apply it?

The future of the Anglican Communion hinges on our ability to answer these deeper questions. Thankfully, we have within our shared past a vast wealth of resources on which to draw in this necessary conversation. It has been some five hundred years since the dawn of the English Reformation, that fractured, fruitful season in the life of Western Christendom during which the Church in England carved out an identity for itself vis-à-vis the Church of Rome and other emerging reform movements in western Europe.

During that period one of the clarion calls of the Reformers was *ad fontes*, which can be loosely translated as "to the sources." It was a cry that reflected the Reformers' intent to delve deeply into the text of Scripture and the interpretive traditions of the early church fathers in an effort to answer many of the same basic questions that confront the church today. This volume, the first in a planned library of six, responds to the call *ad fontes* in a particularly twenty-first-century way, by returning to the founding documents of the English Reformation and considering the ways in which we answered these basic questions at the dawn of our now global communion. Within these founding formularies a well-refined and theologically rich vision emerges, one that is rooted in Scripture and aligned with the teachings of the early church. It is a vision we believe is capable of reinvigorating our global communion and providing clarity in the midst of mass confusion over our shared identity. Furthermore, we believe that the rich theological heritage of the Reformation is able to give us practical guidance on life and ministry in this twenty-first century.

Therefore, this volume can be divided into three parts. Chapter 1 opens with a sweeping historic narrative of the missionary birth of the church in England, the maturing of English Christianity during the Reformation, and the expansion of this renewed apostolic faith through overseas missions in the five centuries that have followed. From this high-altitude vantage point we descend in chapter 2 to a grassroots perspective to examine the age of the Reformation and the chief personality at the center of the English Reformation: Thomas Cranmer. Here we introduce the Anglican Formularies and the theological convictions that lie at their core. These core beliefs, captured in four Latin slogans of the Reformation, provide the structure for the second half of the book. Chapters 3 through 6 examine Anglicanism's bedrock theological principles: *sola Scriptura*, *sola gratia*, *sola fide*, and *soli Deo gloria*. Finally, the book concludes with a manifesto for Reformation Anglicanism as the way forward for the global communion.

This multiauthored volume is representative of the geographic and ethnic diversity of our Anglican Communion. The contributors hail from Pakistan, the United States, Australia, and Nigeria. Two of us serve as pastors in parishes in Australia and the United States, one is an archbishop in Nigeria, one a bishop who has served in both Pakistan and England, and one a research scholar in Germany. The chapters were written independently and retain the unique voices of their authors, but the content is based on extensive conversation and represents our attempt to speak with a single voice, one that makes Reformation Anglicanism accessible and relevant today.

CHAPTER 1

How the Anglican Communion Began and Where It Is Going

Michael Nazir-Ali

The Missionary Birth of the Church of England

Under Roman rule, the island of Britain was a provincial backwater on the very edge of civilization.[1] No cultured Latin, Greek, Syrian, or Egyptian was terribly interested in what happened out on that rain-drenched, druid-filled frontier, let alone in writing down its history. Consequently, the origins of the church in England are now lost in the mists of time.

It seems only logical that Christians who came to Britain with the Roman occupiers first brought the faith to the island. Whether they arrived specifically as missionaries or came primarily for business and ended up sharing their faith with those around them, no one can say. Nor does any information survive as to how quickly

---

1. This chapter is adapted from Michael Nazir-Ali, *How the Anglican Communion Came to Be and Where It Is Going* (London: Latimer, 2013), with permission.

their efforts produced local congregations. The story of the conversion and martyrdom of the native Briton Saint Alban, who perished perhaps as early as the beginning of the third century, indicates the presence of Christianity in the country at that time, albeit in a situation of severe persecution. Even after the withdrawal of Roman military protection and the subsequent Anglo-Saxon invasions of the fifth and sixth centuries, vestiges of the Christian church survived among the Britons, as is clear from the writings of the Anglo-Saxon historian Bede (673–735).[2] However, having felt the sting of their rivals' swords, the island Christians did not feel any obligation to share the faith with their new pagan Germanic neighbors.

That missionary impulse was to come from much farther away, all the way back to Rome, now no longer a ruling imperial city, but still the home of the leading bishop of the Western church. Pope Gregory the Great plucked Augustine from leadership of a comfortable monastery in Rome and sent him to the shores of England, now beyond the edge of civilization, in 597. A reluctant missionary, Augustine had to be encouraged by Gregory to persist in what he had been sent to do. However, his monastery at Canterbury eventually became the mother church for an emergent Anglo-Saxon Christianity throughout the island. Even as the Church of England felt forced to purge itself of medieval corruption and weakness during the sixteenth century, the English Reformers and monarchs continued to respect and honor their missionary debt to the Church of Rome.

At the same time, however, the Reformers pointed out that the church had existed in Britain before the arrival of Augustine and his fellow monks. Archbishop Matthew Parker is typical in claiming a mythic apostolic pedigree for this church.[3] Of course, it is only pure legend that Joseph of Arimathea came to Glastonbury as England's first missionary bishop during the first century. Nevertheless, Au-

---

2. Bede, *The Ecclesiastical History of the English People* (Oxford: Oxford University Press, 2008), 36.

3. See further, Paul Avis, *Anglicanism and the Christian Church* (Edinburgh: T&T Clark, 1989), 24ff.

gustine soon learned that the Celtic church, established long before his arrival, was still active among the British people who had been driven back to western and northern parts of the island by the Anglo-Saxon invaders.

The struggle between Roman and Celtic forms of Christianity, as well as between Britain and Ireland, is often described as if each was mutually exclusive of the other. The usual polarizations, however, are not accurate. After all, Patrick, the founder of Christianity in Ireland, was himself a British Christian. The son of a deacon and the grandson of a priest, he was kidnapped from the west coast of Britain and made a slave to serve across the sea among the pagan Irish. After escaping and returning home six years later, he felt God's call to return to the land of his captors and, since he now spoke Gaelic, preach the gospel to them in their own language. Moreover, during his religious training in Gaul, he became familiar with Roman custom, and this seems to have been the form of the Christian faith that he preached in Ireland. He remained, nevertheless, sensitive to Irish spirituality, acknowledging the significance of woods, springs, and wells, as well as the importance of dreams and visions.

Patrick's missionary zeal and method became part of the spiritual DNA of the Celtic church. As a result, at about the same time that Augustine was arriving in southeast England at Canterbury, the Irish monk Columba had not only settled on the Scottish island of Iona but also made it a center for missionary work in northern England. Paulinus of York and Rochester, a bishop who had been sent out from Canterbury, had converted King Edwin of Northumbria to Christianity. After Edwin had been killed in battle, Paulinus returned south, but left many Roman converts behind. A year later, Oswald, Edwin's nephew, became king of Northumbria. In his youth, Oswald had taken refuge in Scotland, where he was converted to Irish Christianity. When he became king, he invited Aidan to come from Iona and found a monastery on Lindisfarne Island as a base for evangelizing his kingdom.

As a result, in Northumbria the Roman and Celtic churches directly collided. Their competing forms of mission had many aims in common: evangelization, baptism, and Christianization. However, significant differences still divided them. Most importantly, the Roman mission emphasized organizational stability for long-term growth. They fostered a strong institutional life for the church by establishing bishops with specific dioceses, holding synods, and insisting on a common liturgy marked by the same feasts and fasts. The Celts, on the other hand, saw themselves as pilgrims for Christ. Their primary motive was giving up everything, even their homeland, for the sake of following Christ. Their bishops lived in monasteries and made missionary trips out and about to pastor their flocks and increase them.

In short, the Roman missional strategy was to stress founding structures capable of shaping a message, whereas the Celtic way was to proclaim a message with the power to create a community. Yet, even these differences can be emphasized too much. Although the Roman mission placed its highest value on institutional rootedness, pilgrimage remained very important for the progress of the Roman mission in early medieval Northern Europe. Indeed, such Anglo-Saxons as Boniface, who left his homeland in England to become the apostle to Germany, emulated the Irish example.[4]

Because of their substantial differences, however, it should be no surprise that these two ways of living out the life of the church came into conflict. This tension came to a head at the Synod of Whitby (AD 664) and was, according to Bede, largely resolved in favor of Roman customs. Nevertheless, the tension between mission as enduring structure and mission as traveling message has recurred throughout the history of the church. For example, enclosed monasticism like the Benedictines (founded about 530) emphasized stability. During the Middle Ages, however, the new mendicant (i.e., begging) orders arose. As exemplified by the Franciscans and the

---

4. On all of this, see Anton Wessels, *Europe: Was It Ever Really Christian?* (London: SCM, 1994), 55ff.

Dominicans, these new groups emphasized traveling, teaching, and preaching among laypeople.

Of course, these were not the only tensions in the church. Another key issue was the proper relationship between the church and secular governments. Bishops were important figures in society, since they controlled the revenues from large amounts of land given to the church. Who, then, should appoint them: the king or the pope? After much struggle, Rome generally prevailed in this dispute, which became known as the investiture controversy (i.e., Who should "invest" a bishop with his office?). Even a section of the Magna Carta, the first great legal document limiting the powers of English kings, upheld the freedom of the *Ecclesia Anglicana* (the English church). Nevertheless, in practice kings managed increasingly to restrict the church's freedom to act, especially, but not only, in the matter of episcopal appointments.[5] In England, Parliament passed the *Praemunire* law (1392), which prevented interference in the English church from Rome or any other foreign power.

If the church's worldly wealth made kings want to control it, reform movements within the church wanted to remove that temptation by taking the church and its members back to an idealized notion of apostolic simplicity. Saint Francis (1182–1226) and the mendicant order he founded is just one example of these movements. The Franciscans inspired people by their preaching and their practice of evangelical virtues (poverty, chastity, and obedience), as well as by the different ways they lived together as a community. Later on, when their original vigor and rigor had been much weakened by worldliness and internal conflicts over how to be true followers of Francis, they themselves became the objects of attacks by newer reform movements. John Wycliffe (1320–1384), an Oxford doctor of divinity, renewed the call for the church to give up its worldly possessions and power. He emphasized the authority

---

5. Colin Padmore, "The Choosing of Bishops in the Early Church and in the Church of England: An Historical Survey," in *Working with the Spirit: Choosing Diocesan Bishops* (London: Church House, 2001), 113ff.

of Scripture and rejected Roman teachings he thought unbiblical, like transubstantiation and the clergy holding the keys to the forgiveness of sins. To give people a chance to decide for themselves whether Roman teaching was faithful to Scripture, he encouraged the translation of the Bible into English. But the Roman church condemned Wycliffe, his followers (called Lollards), and their translation of the Bible into English as heretical. Consequently, it was illegal to have an English Bible without a license from the bishop up until the reign of Henry VIII.[6]

The fifteenth century also witnessed a massive revival of ancient learning. Encouraged by the development of printing, which made possible the wide availability of books, the Renaissance brought into existence a Christian humanism. This varied from place to place, but it created a love of knowledge, especially about the Bible and the early centuries of Christianity, as well as revulsion at superstition and corruption. It is interesting that Desiderius Erasmus (1466–1536), whose translation of the New Testament triggered so much of the Reformation, was responsible also for a severe critique of popular cults, including that of the Virgin Mary. In his desire to give Mary a truly biblical place in the church, he was joined by others, such as Sir Thomas More.[7]

The early Reformers were quite as exercised about the abuses in the church, and it is instructive to compare the language used by More and Erasmus with that of Tyndale. It is a pity that the polemical climate of the time, and perhaps the temperament of the antagonists, did not allow them to see the common ground among them. This is also true of their desire for the availability of the Scriptures in the vernacular. Erasmus was an advocate not only of reading the Bible in its original languages but also of making it available to the humblest. Without Erasmus's edition of the Greek New Testament

6. Owen Chadwick, *The Reformation* (London: Penguin, 1990), 11ff.; *The Little Flowers of St Francis* (London: Kegan Paul, n.d.).

7. M. Nazir-Ali and N. Sagovsky, "The Virgin Mary in the Anglican Tradition of the 16th and 17th Centuries," in *Studying Mary*, ed. A. Denaux and N. Sagovsky (London: T&T Clark, 2007), 131ff.

and its Latin translation, Tyndale would have been unable to do his work to make the Scriptures available even to "a boye that dryveth the plough." It is to be regretted, though, that there was no generally available English Bible in the pre-Reformation Church of England, despite the endorsement by someone so esteemed by the Tudor establishment as Erasmus.[8]

Mission in the English Reformation

The Reformers were, of course, concerned that individuals should come to be right with God, but they were also keen that people should lead holy lives and that the church should be purified. While the radical Reformation may have looked more to a people called out from among the nations, the mainstream Reformers were thinking of discipling whole nations by bringing God's Word to them. This sense of national mission was clearly manifested when the Church of England declared its independence from Rome in 1534. Seeing the visible church as essentially a human institution, albeit with a divine vocation, the English Reformers accepted that whomever God had appointed to rule a given society had authority not only in secular affairs but also in matters of its institutional church. Hence, in England the monarch should hold supremacy in the religious affairs of the kingdom, not the pope.

The Crown Legislation passed under Henry VIII and Elizabeth I often invoked pre-Reformation provisions like *Praemunire* as justification for rejecting interference in the English church from Rome or elsewhere. Henry took the title of "Supreme Head" of the church and certainly acted the part, closing all the monasteries and issuing his own theological primer known as the King's Book. However, his daughter Elizabeth was much more cautious in her claims. She preferred the more modest title "Supreme Governor" and attached

---

8. See Brian Moynahan, *William Tyndale: If God Spare My Life* (London: Abacus, 2003); William Tyndale, *The Obedience of a Christian Man*, ed. David Daniell (London: Penguin, 2000); Eamon Duffy, *The Stripping of the Altars: Traditional Religion in England c. 1400– c. 1580* (New Haven, CT: Yale University Press, 1992), 53ff.; Chadwick, *The Reformation*, 38–39.

an Admonition to the Royal Injunctions of 1559 that explicitly repudiated any claim to interfere in the ministry of the church. This is
reflected in Article 37 of the Thirty-Nine Articles, which states that
"we give not to our princes the ministering either of God's Word or
of the Sacraments."[9]

For the English Reformers, the goal of such a state-sponsored
Reformation was to use the authority of secular government to
promote biblical faithfulness at every level of their society. They
combined church and state so that the faithful could have the opportunity to evangelize the culture more effectively. They hoped
that such Erastianism (i.e., having a state-directed church) would
promote a thorough proclamation of the gospel throughout English
life so that more people would practice lives of mature Christian
discipleship, and the society as a whole would be better as a result.
We shall take a closer look at their national program for "mission as
proclamation of the message" in the next chapter. However, it must
be said that a merging of church and state also holds out the opposite possibility, that secular culture might corrupt the faith, deform-
ing the church and undermining the Christian way of life. Some
have found Anglicanism's Erastian origins to be its "Achilles' heel."
Indeed, Episcopal theologians Ephraim Radner and Philip Turner
have claimed that their province's capitulation to American culture
in matters like authority, revelation, the uniqueness of Christ, and
human sexuality is a direct result of the sixteenth-century decision to wed church life to contemporary society.[10] We shall need to
examine this issue in more detail later on as well.

But what about Christian mission beyond the British Isles, indeed beyond Europe itself? Did the Church of England have any
interest in promoting the gospel beyond the realm of its monarch?
It has often been said that while the Counter-Reformation fea-

---

9. Avis, *Anglicanism and the Christian Church*, 38–39.
10. Ephraim Radner and Philip Turner, *The Fate of Communion: The Agony of Anglicanism and the Future of a Global Church* (Grand Rapids, MI: Eerdmans, 2006), 2ff.; and
Richard Hooker, *Laws of Ecclesiastical Polity*, ed. Arthur Pollard (Manchester: Fyfield,
1990), bk. 8, 191ff.

tured a great sense of world mission, the Reformation did not. Indeed, it was a common charge against the Reformers that they could make Christians "heretics," but they could not convert the heathen. Of course, their Roman Catholic critics were not necessarily much more effective. Although the papal agreements with Spain and Portugal required every expedition of exploration or conquest to carry chaplains, these efforts were inevitably tainted with the cruelty and greed of the conquistadores.[11] The religious orders were more independent, and while some certainly stood up for the indigenous population, others were implicated in their exploitation and subjugation.[12] In further defense of the Reformers, it can also be legitimately said that the renewal of faith, the teaching of the Bible, worship in the vernacular, and developing a sense of vocation among the laity were the Reformation's focus of mission. Moreover, it should be noted that as long as the sea routes were controlled by Catholic powers, the Protestant nations could not easily engage in world mission.

Such excuses are not enough, however, for as the historian of mission Warneck tells us, no sorrow was expressed in these churches about their inability to engage in mission, and their silence about the missionary task can only be accounted for by the fact that even the *idea* of world mission was absent.[13] Bishop Stephen Neill, similarly, tells us that the thrust of Protestant thought was not that foreign missions would come in God's good time but that they were neither obligatory nor desirable. He further identifies this attitude with the Reformation's emphasis on local or national churches. These not only were contained within specific boundaries but also were confined to particular ethnicities and to the limited vision of local rulers and populations. In addition, there was a kind of dispensationalism

---

11. Michael Nazir-Ali, *From Everywhere to Everywhere: A World View of Christian Mission* (London: Collins, 1990), 38ff.

12. Stephen Neill, *A History of Christian Missions* (London: Penguin, 1990), 145; and Ondina Gonzalez and Justo Gonzalez, *Christianity in Latin America* (New York: Cambridge University Press, 2008), 73ff.

13. G. Warneck, *Outline of a History of Protestant Missions from the Reformation to the Present Time: A Contribution to Modern Church History* (New York: Revell, 1901), 8ff.

among some that held that the gospel had already been preached to all nations. After all, many of them believed they were living in the last days before Christ's imminent return. There was no need to reach out in evangelism again to those who had refused it before.[14]

There were exceptions, of course, and Neill records some, among them Adrian Saravia (1532–1613), the Dutch Protestant who became an Anglican and eventually a canon of Westminster (some say dean). Saravia believed that the missionary mandate was for every age because it was accompanied by our Lord's promise to be with his church to the very end. Such a promise has never been understood to mean he would be with the apostles only, and so the command to which the promise is attached could not be limited to the apostolic band either. The apostles, moreover, had chosen fellow workers and successors to continue their work. As a matter of fact, the church's missionary work had continued through the years, and the gospel had challenged more and more people, who responded to it in different ways. Saravia expressly related his understanding of the continuing missionary mandate of the church to the doctrine of apostolic succession: bishops were successors of the apostles not only as chief pastors but also as leaders in mission. He was vigorously attacked on the continent both for his teaching on mission and for his view on episcopacy, but he remains, for Anglicans, an early champion of world mission.[15]

In spite of Saravia's courageous upholding of mission, it has to be admitted that Anglicanism displayed the same lack of interest in world mission as other churches of the Reformation. Even though the 1662 Book of Common Prayer provided a rite for the baptism of "such as are of Riper Years" as useful for the baptizing of "Natives in our Plantations, and others converted to the Faith," Neill can find records for only one Indian being baptized according to Anglican rites in the whole of the seventeenth century.[16]

---

14. Neill, *A History of Christian Missions*, 187–88.
15. Ibid., 189; Nazir-Ali, *From Everywhere to Everywhere*, 43ff.
16. Neill, *A History of Christian Missions*, 197–98.

The Emergence of Anglican Missionary Societies

So how *did* Anglicanism become global? How is it there is a world-wide Anglican Communion today which is one of the most widely spread Christian traditions, even if not the most numerous? In fact, there is no single answer to these questions. The Anglican tradition became global in a number of ways. There was, first of all, what we might call the *coincidental* spread of Anglican churches. Like the initial arrival of Christianity in Roman Britain, Anglicanism's incipient global spread was coincidental in the strictest meaning of that term: the Church of England simply accompanied the colonization and settlement by the British of lands in North America, the Caribbean, Africa, Asia, Australasia, and so on. The colonists naturally took their church with them and generally made every effort to see that it resembled the church at home as much as possible. Thereby hangs a tale.

Nevertheless, at the same time, a second, more intentional method arose, the missionary society movement. The earliest two groups were the Society for Promoting Christian Knowledge (SPCK, 1698) and the Society for the Propagation of the Gospel (SPG, 1701). Their first aim was to provide for the pastoral care of British people overseas, but it was also their desire to bring other peoples, living within British dominions, to the Christian faith. Neill records some of the achievements of the German missionaries who worked with these societies of high church convictions. They ministered according to the Anglican rite and Anglican discipline but never received episcopal ordination. SPCK provided the press on which the first Tamil New Testament was printed, and it was a SPG-sponsored young man, Philip Quaque, who became, in 1765, the first African to receive holy orders according to the Anglican Ordinal.[17]

One hundred years later, the desire for cross-cultural mission, already implicit in the vision of SPCK and SPG, received a huge impetus with the emergence of the Church Missionary Society

---

17. Ibid.

(CMS, 1799) as a result of the evangelical revival. The eighteenth century was a time of great change and even of turmoil in Britain, but it was also an exciting time. The preaching of George White-field (1714–1770) and John Wesley (1703–1791) had warmed the hearts of many. Bibles were being opened and read with the realization that God's purposes were universal and that the gospel had, indeed, to be preached to "every creature." Both the evangelicals' Bible reading and Enlightenment thought about the dignity of the person led many to view the slave trade and the institution of slavery with increasing revulsion. But the Bible also inspired a fresh commitment to the worldwide mission of the church. It is no accident that the Clapham Sect, a group of Anglican evangelicals, had among their projects not only the abolition of the hated slave trade and slavery itself but also the establishing of a "model colony" of freed slaves in Sierra Leone. They were also, of course, engaged in improving the condition of the poor in Britain through education, laying the groundwork for industrial legislation by their successors, and in what they described as "the reformation of manners." The formation of the CMS has to be seen against this background of a Christian mission, influenced by the Enlightenment, but drawing its basic inspiration from the Bible.[18]

From the very beginning the emphasis was on preaching the gospel, bringing people to personal faith in Jesus Christ, and on the emergence of Christian communities that would be self-support-ing, self-governing, and self-propagating. Henry Venn, its secretary from 1841 to 1872, is usually credited—along with Rufus Ander-son, the American mission strategist of the same period, and then later Roland Allen, from a more high church background—with the formulation and development of this "three-self" principle. As Peter Williams has shown, however, they were not unique in such

---

18. As the background to all of this, see David Bebbington, *Evangelicalism in Modern Brit-ain* (London: Unwin Hyman, 1989); Kevin Ward and Brian Stanley, eds., *The Church Mission Society and World Christianity, 1799–1999* (Grand Rapids, MI: Eerdmans, 2000); Jocelyn Murray, *Proclaim the Good News: A Short History of the Church Missionary Society* (London: Hodder & Stoughton, 1985).

thinking, as other Anglicans, Protestants, and Roman Catholics also thought in similar ways.[19] Where the CMS had to work, by compulsion or by choice, either with the ancient churches, as in India with the Orthodox, or with establishment Anglicanism, it sought the renewal of the church in worship, theological education, and holiness of life.

In the Anglican context, however, CMS did insist on the priority of the community over the need for bishops. In a characteristic dispute with the Anglo-Catholic Tractarians, it rejected the need for ecclesiastical authorities to send "missionary bishops" who would then establish a church with clergy, appropriate church government, discipline, and so on. The simple proclamation of the gospel was sufficient to create a Christian community whose life together would then be structured for best missional effectiveness in the local context. As Williams has shown, this ideal was compromised from time to time, but it remained a basic ecclesiological difference between CMS and the more high church societies, such as SPG and the Universities Mission to Central Africa (UMCA), as well as with colonial bishops like Bishop G. S. Selwyn of New Zealand and then of Lichfield. It cannot be claimed that CMS's motives in promoting such an ecclesiology were entirely disinterested. CMS feared the appointment of high church bishops and the possible curtailment of its own role as a voluntary mission organization. How ironic, therefore, that the first appointment of missionary bishops in our own times should take place in Nigeria, one of the first areas of operation for the CMS.[20]

Venn and, therefore, CMS were firm advocates of the emergence of independent national churches that should enjoy the closest spiritual relations with the Church of England but should otherwise be responsible for their own worship, discipline, and order.[21] In this

---

19. Peter Williams, *The Ideal of the Self-Governing Church: A Study in Victorian Missionary Strategy* (Leiden: Brill, 1990), 1ff.

20. Ibid., 11ff.

21. Peter Williams, "'Not Transplanting': Henry Venn's Strategic Vision," in Ward and Stanley, *The Church Mission Society and World Christianity*, 147ff.

sense, they sowed the idea of autonomy, which both characterizes contemporary Anglicanism and has become its leading problem.

Almost from the beginning, the evangelical movement had a vigorous debate about the nature of the Bible. All agreed that the Bible was, indeed, the inspired Word of God but differed in their understanding of such inspiration and its extent. Thus, some could, and did, refer to it as "the infallible Word of God." Then there were those, like Philip Doddridge, who distinguished between different degrees of inspiration as, for him, some parts afforded a greater insight into the divine mind than others. And, yet again, there were those, such as Henry Martyn, the well-known missionary and translator, who explained to a Muslim interlocutor that, in contrast to what Muslims believed about the Qur'an, he believed that, for the Bible, the "sense was from God but the expression from the different writers of it." The fault lines were thus laid for the bitter controversy that was to break out from time to time.[22]

There were several periods and aspects to this controversy, but, for our purposes, it was the division within CMS (sometimes called "the barometer" of Anglican evangelicalism) that is relevant. There was, first of all, the direct issue of the historical trustworthiness of the Scriptures. A significant number of the CMS membership felt that missionary candidates should be made to subscribe to some formula that expressed this clearly. Others, including CMS staff, held that candidates should not be asked to believe in anything beyond the formularies of the Church of England. Behind this lay the ubiquitous issue of "Anglican comprehensiveness." Should CMS strive to be as comprehensive as the Anglican Church and, if not, what were the limits?

In the end, a formula could not be found to keep both sides together, and this led to the formation of the Bible Churchmen's Missionary Society (BCMS), consisting of those who wished to uphold the trustworthiness of Scripture in every respect and not just in

---

22. Bebbington, *Evangelicalism in Modern Britain*, 12–13, 86–87.

matters of faith. This division in evangelical missionary ranks was a heavy blow at the time, but, in due course, the formation of the BCMS provided another opening for those wanting to engage in world mission. BCMS set out to be a pioneer in a number of areas and eventually some of its work became complementary to CMS. Much of the bitterness was forgotten, but the question about the nature and extent of biblical authority still lurked in the background.[23]

An important aspect of mission and the evangelical revival is its voluntary nature. The labors of the Clapham Sect, the rise of CMS, and other features of the revival can perhaps best be described as expressions of a voluntary movement of Christians concerned for justice and freedom—for instance, with regard to slavery and the working conditions of men, women, and children—but also for bringing the gospel to people both at home and abroad. The CMS was always keen to emphasize the "Church" aspect of its identity, and the wider church's approval is shown by the fact that, throughout the nineteenth century, more and more bishops agreed to become vice-presidents of the society.[24] At the same time, CMS and other organizations also wished to affirm the voluntary nature of their calling, which distinguished them from, for example, the high church SPG, which had been established by convocation and by royal charter. At a time when institutional provision seems to be failing the church, the idea of men and women being called by God for mission and ministry is becoming attractive once again. It is very instructive, in this context, to consider the history of voluntary movements in the Anglican Communion and the wider church.

The older missionary societies, SPCK and SPG, were founded on high church (rather than CMS "Church") principles; but, as Bishop Neill points out, until 1861 they had no scruples over employing non-episcopally ordained German Lutherans to minister according to the Anglican rite in the areas of their mission activity.[25]

23. Ibid., 217–18; and, Murray, *Proclaim the Good News*, 177ff.
24. Williams, *The Ideal of the Self-Governing Church*, 14n118.
25. Neill, *A History of Christian Missions*, 198–99.

This would not be possible after the Tractarian movement began in the Church of England.

One of its more recent historians, Bishop John Davies, comments that mission was not, at first, a priority for the leaders and thinkers of the Oxford movement. They were more concerned with questions about the nature of the church and its relations with the state, and with the sacraments and the ministry that made them possible. Already in the early period, however, leaders like Hurrell Froude and John Henry Newman were becoming attracted to the idea of being missionary bishops abroad where they could develop their ideas about the church and its oversight free of what they regarded as the Erastian constraints of England.[26]

The real catalyst was David Livingstone's speech at the Senate House in Cambridge in 1857. Among other things, it led to the formation of the Universities Mission to Central Africa. It is, indeed, remarkable that such an Anglo-Catholic mission should have begun under the inspiration of, and with the actual assistance of, a Scottish Congregationalist. The mission was, from the beginning, characterized by an emphasis on missionary bishops and on seeing the church as, first and foremost, a spiritual society. It was active against slavery and, as Neill reminds us in his book on Anglicanism, no one can fail to be moved when they see the cathedral in Zanzibar built on the very site of the old slave market with its sanctuary where the whipping post had been. It is interesting to note, in this context, that the first African to be ordained as a result of the mission's work was a former slave of the Sultan of Zanzibar.[27]

The SPG was also gradually "catholicized" and became, in many ways, characteristic of Catholic Anglican mission values. The merger of the two societies in 1965 to form the United Society for the Propagation of the Gospel can be seen as a kind of watershed in the story of Anglican Catholic mission. In 2015, to reflect its com-

---

26. Williams, *The Ideal of the Self-Governing Church*, 13–14; John D. Davies, *The Faith Abroad* (Oxford: Blackwells, 1983), 1ff.

27. Stephen Neill, *Anglicanism* (Harmondsworth, Middlesex: Penguin, 1958), 342–43; and Neill, *A History of Christian Missions*, 265ff., 323ff.

mitment to mission as partnership and evangelism as inclusion, the organization changed the meaning of its acronym to stand for United Society Partners in the Gospel.

In summary, then, Anglicanism became a worldwide communion in at least three quite distinct ways. First, it spread *coincidentally* (in the strict sense of that term) alongside the movements of English-speaking peoples across the world: into the Americas, the Caribbean, Africa, Asia, and the Pacific. As these people went to new lands, they took their church with them. Not only were buildings and architecture transplanted, but also ways of worship, styles of church government, the temper of pastoral care, and so on. In some parts of the world, the tendency to replicate what was at "home" was more pronounced than in others; but, on the whole, this kind of Anglicanism looked much like its mother, the Church of England, even when events like the American Revolution modified some of its features.

Second, another great force was *evangelical revival* and the birth of societies like the CMS and Church's Ministry among the Jewish People, and the participation of Anglicans in interdenominational ventures, such as the British and Foreign Bible Society. The emphasis here was on personal conversion, the planting of Christian communities, and the centrality of the Word of God. Church order was deemed secondary and was to follow the establishing of churches through proclamation. The aim was that these should be self-supporting, self-governing, and self-propagating.[28] Evangelical Anglicans were willing to enter into "comity" arrangements with non-Episcopal churches, and these arrangements still determine the ecclesiastical map of many countries in Africa and elsewhere.[29] They also became the occasion for discussions about greater Christian unity and led, in some places, to schemes for united churches.

Third, the Anglican Catholic missions like SPG and the

---

28. See, further, Bebbington, *Evangelicalism in Modern Britain*, 2ff.; and Williams, *The Ideal of the Self-Governing Church*, 2ff. and passim.

29. Neill, *A History of Christian Missions*, 401; Murray, *Proclaim the Good News*, 170–71.

Universities Mission to Central Africa sought to promote a more distinctly spiritual, high church understanding of Anglicanism. In contradistinction to the evangelicals, these societies were concerned to uphold the distinctiveness of Anglican church order and tended to see world mission as a way of establishing authentic "catholic" order in the unambiguous way that was not possible in the established church back in England. Their concern for the church's freedom and their belief that it was primarily a spiritual society had led Anglo-Catholics from the very beginning to be suspicious of, even hostile to, the establishment of the Church of England as the official state religion.[30]

Traditions of Dissent from the State in Anglicanism

Thus, from its earliest days, the *Ecclesia Anglicana* has had two ecclesiological streams: the church as a community formed from the proclamation of the gospel of Jesus Christ versus the church as a set of distinctly sacred institutional structures centered on its bishops who represent an unbroken chain of authority and empowerment traceable back to Christ's apostles. The English Reformers favored the former understanding, choosing to merge the structures of the church with those of the secular government for the sake of the Christian message's more thorough enculturation in English society, though this did not deny the apostolic foundation of the church. Later high church Anglicans felt increasingly uncomfortable with this understanding. They sought to reinterpret the Church of England as a divinely instituted sacred society, separate and distinct from the secular government and society it sought to serve.

Despite the Reformers' intention of promoting revolutionary change through establishment, it cannot be denied that the Church of England's relation to the state has often encouraged a theology and praxis that legitimizes the status quo. There are, undoubtedly, those in both church and state who regard establishment as a li-

---

30. Davies, *The Faith Abroad*, 42ff.

cense by the state for the church to exist and to enjoy certain social privileges. Nicholls and Williams point out that this was certainly not the original meaning of being established by law, however it may have come to be understood through the centuries.[31]

Many are surprised to learn, then, that there are in fact well-established traditions of being prophetic and even of dissent from the state within Anglicanism. Whether this has to do with Saint Anselm's insistence that Henry I should take an oath to maintain the liberties of his subjects before he could be crowned, or with Saint Thomas Becket's sacrificial championing of the church's freedoms, which led to his death, or with Stephen Langton's leadership against King John in upholding Magna Carta, we see how principled resistance could take place in the pre-Reformation *Ecclesia Anglicana*. At the time of Henry VIII's claim to royal supremacy over the church, the not-wholly-courageous convocations initially accepted Henry's claims only "insofar as the law of Christ allows." The martyrdoms on both sides of the Reformation divide showed how people of every rank were prepared to suffer and even to die for their convictions.[32]

The Puritans did not believe that either Edward VI or Elizabeth had completed the task of the Reformation. In this sense, they wanted the Reformation to continue until the church had been purged of all corruption, error, and idolatry. Nothing should be done that was not explicitly laid down in the Bible, and they wished such high-mindedness not only for the church but also, by force of law, for society at large. Many resented their austere view of the Christian life, and this no doubt accounts for the pejorative way in which the term *puritan* is understood today. This is not the place to critique their agenda, save to say that it inevitably involved them in resisting and opposing authority.[33]

---

31. David Nicholls and Rowan Williams, *Politics and Theological Identity* (London: Jubilee Group, 1984).

32. On all of this, see further Catherine Glass and David Abbott, *Share the Inheritance* (Shawford: Inheritance, 2010), 33ff.; Chadwick, *The Reformation*, 99–100, 125ff.

33. Chadwick, *The Reformation*, 175ff.; and A. M. Renwick and A. M. Harman, *The Story of the Church* (Nottingham: Inter-Varsity Press, 2009), 130ff.

In many ways, the Non-Jurors were the exact opposite of the Puritans. They were high churchmen who also believed in the divine right of kings. Paradoxically, it was this very doctrine that brought them into conflict with the state and the monarch after the Glorious Revolution of 1688. Having taken oaths of allegiance to the overthrown James II and his successors, they were unable to take even modified oaths to the newly arrived William and Mary. Because of this, the bishops (including the archbishop of Canterbury) and the clergy among them were deprived of their sees or their livings by Parliament without there ever having been canonical proceedings against them. Some formed communities of their own, while others continued to worship in their parishes, even if they were unable to hold any office in the official Church of England. Some of the bishops wished to ensure ministerial succession, since they increasingly saw the official church as hopelessly compromised. They also desired to worship in the way they imagined the "primitive" Christian communities to have done. Eventually, they produced a eucharistic rite which showed signs of Eastern influence (as they were also engaged in negotiations for union with the Eastern churches). This rite influenced the liturgical tradition of the Scottish Episcopal Church and, through it, has been significantly influential in other parts of the Anglican Communion, thus providing an alternative liturgical tradition to the English Book of Common Prayer.

The Non-Jurors were not just scrupulous about their oaths. Their negotiations with the Orthodox reveal their sense that they belonged to a worldwide church and that this somehow had to be visible. They believed the church to be a distinct spiritual society, which, while owing obedience to the state, could not obey if the state demanded something contrary to God's law and its own integrity.[34]

As we have seen, the Tractarian movement in Oxford also arose because of unease with the state's intervention in the affairs of the

---

34. Nazir-Ali, *From Everywhere to Everywhere*, 51–52.

church. Its prophetic stance, however, went beyond the assertion of the church's independence vis-à-vis the state. It extended to crossing social and cultural boundaries, especially to working among the poor. The work of priests like Father Charles Lowder in the East End of London is well known. Alongside them were orders of nuns like the All Saints' Sisters of the Poor and the Sisters of St John the Divine, now made famous by the BBC's series *Call the Midwife.* Although such work could simply be ameliorating the lot of the poor and, at times, could be naïve and patronizing, there was no doubt about their commitment to live among the poor and to bring their plight to the attention of those who had the power to change it for the better. It is also undoubtedly the case that some struggled for justice for the poor and suffered for it.[35]

Although the prophetic aspect of Catholic Anglicanism has receded somewhat in the United Kingdom in recent years, it has been to the fore elsewhere. For example, at least part of the cause of the church of the Province of Southern Africa's stand against colonialism, civil war, and, in particular, the abhorrent doctrine of apartheid was the Catholic background and formation of that church.

We can see, then, that although there *are* elements in Anglicanism that can lead to compromise with and capitulation to culture and to the demands of the State, other forces can provide the wherewithal for resistance and a countercultural stance, if such action becomes necessary.

Anglican Ecclesiology in Practice

The different strands of Anglicanism were to be found side by side in some parts of the world. In India, for example, there was, first of all, the Ecclesiastical Department of the Government of India. The bishops were "Crown" bishops, and their task, with their clergy,

---

35. See Nicholls and Williams, *Politics and Theological Identity*, 19–20; Lawrence Osborn, "Care and Change in Our Society," in *Celebrating the Anglican Way*, ed. Ian Bunting (London: Hodder, 1996), 174; Peter Mayhew, *All Saints: Birth and Growth of a Community* (Oxford: All Saints, 1987); and Jennifer Worth, *In the Midst of Life* (London: Phoenix, 2010).

was to look after the British in India: civil servants, soldiers, traders, and so on, as well as a growing Anglo-Indian population. Large churches, in Gothic or Anglo-Moorish style, were built in the European areas of towns and cities, particularly the cantonments. The churches reflected the might and the wealth of the Raj but have now to be maintained by denominations and congregations that are much poorer. Some of the chaplains did have a burden for reaching out to Indians, but that was not their primary responsibility. There was then the "evangelical" wing of Anglicanism, with churches and institutions emphasizing not only the necessity of personal conversion but also the centrality of the congregation in the life and mission of the church. This was accompanied by the more "Catholic" presence of the SPG, with an emphasis on an apostolic ministry, the contextualization of liturgy, and the centrality of the bishop in the church's work. Bishop Stephen Neill has noted how the two societies worked side by side, with tensions and rivalries but also with a spirit of cooperation and partnership.[36]

India was not alone in having these different expressions of Anglicanism present at the same time and, sometimes, in the same place. In some cases the situation was even more polarized. In what is now Tanzania, for instance, the Anglo-Catholic UMCA evangelized some parts and the avowedly evangelical BCMS evangelized other parts of the area.

When it came to "diocesanization" and later "provincialization," these different expressions had to be brought together into a coherent whole. Constitutions had to be agreed upon, canons promulgated, and liturgies produced that would reflect each of the traditions but would also be rooted in history and, most importantly, in the culture of the peoples to whom the church ministered. In different parts of the world, these processes were not without pain; but in the end, they provided a recognizable Anglicanism that was yet aware of its diverse cultural settings.[37]

---

36. Neill, *A History of Christian Missions*, 232.
37. See Michael Nazir-Ali, "The Vocation of Anglicanism," *Anvil* 6, no. 2 (1989): 115–16.

There continues to be vigorous debate about the basic unit of the church. Is it the congregation, the bishop with clergy and people (the diocese), or is it a province (like the Church of England, Nigeria, etc.)? In the Church of England, the size and the bureaucratic nature of the diocese work against it being seen as an effective ecclesiastical expression. Congregations, especially large evangelical ones, are pressing their claims more and more to being regarded as the basic unit of the church. They claim they have all the elements of preaching the pure Word of God, the administration of the sacraments, and ministries of oversight to be regarded as such.

In the New Testament, the church of God in Corinth, Ephesus, or Rome certainly appears to be a basic way of referring to the church: all of God's people gathered together in a particular locality (while, at the same time, recognizing groups of Christians affiliated with particular households; thus in the letters to the Romans and the Colossians, Saint Paul can ask the wider church to greet the church in the house of Prisca and Aquila, and in that of Nympha). The letters of Ignatius show that early in the second century, in at least some parts, bishops gathering with clergy and people had become a basic way of understanding the church, though we must remember that we are still speaking of a single town-wide congregation.

The New Testament also recognizes the affinity which churches in a region may have for one another (Acts 9:31; 2 Corinthians 8; Col. 4:16; 1 Pet. 1:1; Rev. 1:4; etc.). This, in fact, may be the germ of the provincial idea later developed in the East in the sense of bishops grouped around a metropolitan and in the West in the form, for instance, of the North African church. The former development is attested to in the canons of the Council of Nicaea, and the latter in the letters of Cyprian, especially to successive bishops of Rome.[38]

I have often had cause to remark how Anglicanism at its best, whether deliberately or accidentally, can display a "Cyprianic"

---

38. W. H. C. Frend, *The Early Church* (London: Hodder, 1965), 154–55; Robert B. Eno, *Teaching Authority in the Early Church* (Wilmington, DE: Glazier, 1984), 84–85.

ecclesiology, which emphasizes not only the unity and equality of the bishops but also the proper autonomy of provinces without, however, jeopardizing the communion that local churches need if they are authentically to be "church" with churches throughout the world.

The Reformation in England had rejected Cyprian's view that the see of Rome was, at least, the means of establishing communion among the churches and had firmly established the principle of provincial autonomy. As the Anglican Communion emerged, however, questions arose as to how it was to be held together. The development of the so-called Instruments of Communion came about as an answer to this question.

Anglican Unity

The archbishop of Canterbury has always been seen as *primus inter pares* (first among equals) in the worldwide Anglican college of bishops. As such, he is able to gather together the bishops of the communion. When bishops in Canada, the United States, the Caribbean, and South Africa petitioned for a synodical gathering, the archbishop of Canterbury responded by summoning the first Lambeth Conference in 1867. For reasons largely to do with the establishment of the English church, he could not summon a proper synod but rather convened a somewhat attenuated meeting for "brotherly counsel and encouragement."[39] Since then, the conferences have had, nevertheless, a significant influence within the communion and beyond. Thus, the 1888 conference formulated the definitive version of the Chicago-Lambeth Quadrilateral that set out the basis for Christian unity as being the final authority of the Bible, the catholic creeds, the dominical sacraments of baptism and the Supper of the Lord, and the apostolic ministry.[40]

---

39. Neill, *Anglicanism*, 358ff.; and Alan Stephenson, *Anglicanism and the Lambeth Conferences* (London: SPCK, 1978), 30ff.

40. See G. R. Evans and J. Robert Wright, *The Anglican Tradition: A Handbook of Sources* (London: SPCK, 1991), 354–55.

It is impossible to overstate the importance of the Quadrilateral not only in Anglican negotiations with other churches, especially after Lambeth 1920's *Appeal to All Christian People*, but also in the wider Christian body generally. It cannot be imagined that the schemes for organic unity, such as that in South Asia, West and East Africa, England, and Wales could even have been drawn up, let alone come to fruition as they did in South Asia, without this short but definite formula. Its influence is not, however, limited to such schemes but extends to the Faith and Order movement more generally and, in particular, to documents such as the Lima Text: *Baptism, Eucharist and Ministry* of the World Council of Churches' Faith and Order Commission.[41] More latterly, as Bishop Arthur Vogel has pointed out, the Quadrilateral has increasingly been seen not just as a "yardstick" that Anglicans apply to ecumenical discussions but also as a "mirror" that shows up our own shortcomings and what we are called to be as a communion of churches.[42]

As we have seen, Lambeth Conferences have provided ecumenical guidance about schemes for unity with other Christian traditions, but they have also become important for evaluating bilateral ecumenical agreements such as the Anglican–Roman Catholic International Commission's (ARCIC) Final Report.[43] Nearly every conference until 2008 also provided some spiritual and moral guidance on a crucial issue of Christian living, whether it was contraception (1930), racial discrimination (1948), or the family (1958), right up to 1998 on human sexuality. It is sad to record that the 2008 conference was not allowed to offer any guidance or to make

---

41. On church union, see ibid., 412–13; W. J. Marshall, *Faith and Order in the North India/ Pakistan Unity Plan* (London: Friends of the CNI, 1978); and *Ministry in a Uniting Church* (Swansea: Commission of the Covenanted Churches in Wales, 1986). On the wider influence, see Günter Gassmann, "Quadrilateral, Organic Unity and the WCC Faith and Order Movement," in *Quadrilateral at One Hundred*, ed. J. Robert Wright (Cincinnati, OH: Forward Movement, 1988). For the Lima Text, see "Baptism, Eucharist and Ministry" (Faith and Order Paper no. 111, World Council of Churches, Geneva, 1982).

42. In Wright, *Quadrilateral at One Hundred*, 126ff.

43. See, for instance, the report of the Lambeth Conference 1988, *The Truth Shall Make You Free* (London: ACC, 1988), res. 8, pp. 210–11.

any decisions, thus interrupting the flow of doctrinal, personal, and social teaching.[44]

The Lambeth Consultative Body was a meeting of bishops representing their respective provinces and churches that went back to the Lambeth Conference of 1897. It was to meet yearly and would provide for continuity between Lambeth Conferences. In addition, the 1948 conference recommended the setting up of an Advisory Council on Missionary Strategy. Both the Primates' Meeting, as one of the Instruments of Communion, and the Anglican Consultative Council (ACC) have emerged as a result of these bodies.[45]

The ACC is a strange animal. Its membership consists of bishops, clergy, and laypeople nominated by each province in proportion to its size, but it is not itself synodically constituted. That is, it does not have "houses" for bishops, clergy, and laity that could exercise a role proper to them in making decisions, particularly about the doctrine, worship, order, and moral teaching of the church.[46]

At the same time, we need to note that both the 1988 and the 1998 Lambeth Conferences, sensing the need for greater spiritual and moral guidance for the communion, had asked for an enhanced role for the Primates' Meeting.[47] The Windsor Report recognized this special role for the Primates, as did the earlier drafts of the ill-fated Anglican Covenant. Under pressure, however, from the very provinces that had made the drafting of a covenant necessary, this was abandoned and replaced by a process that would, once again, make effective discipline virtually impossible.[48]

For the 2008 Lambeth Conference, the archbishop of Canterbury was unable to gather all the bishops, since more than a third

---

44. Roger Coleman, ed., *Resolutions of the Twelve Lambeth Conferences: 1867–1988* (Toronto: Anglican Book Centre, 1992).

45. Stephenson, *Anglicanism and the Lambeth Conferences*, 122–23, 252–53.

46. Coleman, *Resolutions of the Twelve Lambeth Conferences*, 171–72.

47. *The Truth Shall Make You Free*, res. 18, p. 216; and *The Official Report of the Lambeth Conference 1998* (Harrisburg, PA: Morehouse, 1999), res. 3.6, pp. 396–97.

48. *The Windsor Report* (London: Anglican Communion Office, 2004), 77ff. See also "The Church of England's Response," in Michael Nazir-Ali and John Hind, *The Windsor Report, GS 1570* (London: Archbishops' Council, 2005); and Andrew Goddard, "The Anglican Communion Covenant," in *Companion to the Anglican Communion*, ed. Ian S. Markham et al. (Malden, MA: Wiley-Blackwell, 2013), 119ff.

refused to come because those bishops who had laid hands on a person living in a same-sex partnership, to make him a bishop, had also been invited with no requirement to express regret or repentance for their actions. A significant number of Primates now refuse to attend Primates' Meetings for similar reasons, thus making it impossible for such meetings to be held. Again, for principled reasons, a number of Primates, bishops, and laypeople have resigned from the Anglican Consultative Council and the Joint Standing Committee of the ACC and the Primates' Meeting.

The result of all of this has been that none of the "Instruments of Communion" developed to sustain and promote the life of the Anglican Communion are now working as intended. Should people, then, simply "learn to walk apart," as Windsor warned, each province or even diocese looking to its own needs and opportunities? This is very far from the Mutual Responsibility and Interdependence (MRI) and the Partners in Mission processes, which have so far characterized our common life together.[49]

Those Anglicans in every province who wish to uphold the authority of the Bible, the historic faith of the church through the ages, and the continuity of apostolic order have had to find ways of associating and of moving forward in the context of a confused worldwide communion. Movements such as The Global Anglican Future Conference (GAFCON) and the more diverse Global South, along with Catholic Anglican organizations like Forward in Faith, have come into existence to ensure that traditional understandings of Anglicanism are not simply extinguished under revisionist pressure.

We have been fortunate enough to inherit both the sacred deposit of faith (of which Scripture is the norm) and a historic ministry that is tasked with preaching the "pure Word of God" and duly celebrating the sacraments of the church. In the history of the church, there have been tendencies to overemphasize one or

---

49. *The Windsor Report*, 75; and Coleman, *Resolutions of the Twelve Lambeth Conferences*, 171ff. etc.

another of these features of the church—and this can result in complacency, faithlessness, division, or inaction. We need to adhere to both of these aspects of our faith and life while, at the same time, being quite clear that they are not on the same level. Although ministers are called of God and minister in his name, they are, nevertheless, always servants of the Word of God and never its masters.[50]

As we struggle to find fresh ways of expressing ourselves as "church" or as a "communion," we need to keep in mind what should characterize our life together. We need to find ways of gathering at every level of the church's life, whether in the parish, at home, as a diocese or a national church, or, indeed, across the communion and worldwide. Naturally, such gatherings will be more than just meeting. They must be gatherings where the Word of God is at the center. They will be prayerful, and they will be eucharistic in the sense that we gather to give thanks for all God's goodness to us and to everyone, but specifically for his "inestimable love in the redemption of the world by Our Lord Jesus Christ," as we say in the General Thanksgiving. When necessary, they will be about consulting one another regarding weighty matters confronting church and society. There will be times when the teaching of the Bible and the church has to be clearly set out, to build up believers and as a witness to the world. Yes, there will also be occasions when the gathering is for the sake of discipline, right doctrine, and holy order in the church.

The Way Forward

We have seen how mission in the course of history has often come about through movements of people responding to God's call on their lives. The monastic movement in both East and West has been about the necessity of prayer, contemplation, simplicity, and utter devotion, but it has also been about mission. Both individuals and religious orders have carried the faith far and wide. Mis-

---

50. See particularly Articles 20 and 26 of the Articles of Religion and *Dei Verbum*, 10, Vatican 2, in Austin Flannery OP, *Vatican Council II* (New York: Costello, 1987), 755–56.

takes have been made, but there have also been courage, sacrifice, and the extension of the kingdom of God through presence and proclamation.[51]

The evangelical revival resulted, among other things, in a recovery of the doctrine of means: that God uses human beings and their resources to further his work. This then brought about a veritable explosion of missionary concern and vocations to worldwide and cross-cultural missions, which under God, has changed the map of the Christian world.[52]

Anglicans too have been influenced by the voluntary principle, both in their participation in interdenominational missionary activity and in the use of specifically Anglican societies like the CMS, Church's Ministry among the Jewish People, and, later, BCMS. We have seen also how the Tractarian movement became interested in mission because of the possibility of missionary bishops planting churches that were more clearly catholic than the Erastianism of the Church of England would permit. Both CMS and UMCA, in different ways and at different times, became involved in campaigns against the slave trade and slavery itself. This gave a prophetic edge to their witness from the very beginning. Such a prophetic aspect to mission has been seen through the years, whether in the opposition to the caste system in India, the cause of female education, or the resistance to racial segregation and apartheid in South Africa.

Once again, it is very likely that the renewal of Anglicanism will come about not through the reform of structures (necessary as that is) or through institutional means but through movements, raised up by God. These can be mission movements for planting churches among the unreached or movements for renewal in worship and for the receiving and using of God's gifts for the people. They can be campaigners for justice for the poor or for the persecuted. In many

51. See, further, Neill, *Anglicanism*, 179ff.; Timothy (Kallistos) Ware, *The Orthodox Church* (Harmondsworth, Middlesex: Penguin, 1973), 82ff.; W. G. Young, *Patriarch, Shah and Caliph* (Rawalpindi: Christian Study Centre, 1974), 121ff.; and Wessels, *Europe: Was It Ever Really Christian?*, 58ff.

52. Nazir-Ali, *From Everywhere to Everywhere*, 46; Bebbington, *Evangelicalism in Modern Britain*, 41.

and varied ways, the gospel will, indeed, renew both the church and the face of the earth. The hope and prayer of this book is that a fresh movement of reformation in Anglicanism will inspire a new generation to give itself fully to this, God's mission among us in the twenty-first century.

CHAPTER 2

The Power of Unconditional Love in the Anglican Reformation

Ashley Null

Any call for a twenty-first-century reformation of the Anglican Communion needs to go, *ad fontes*, back to the reformation movement that birthed the independent English church in the first place. The English Reformation can be described as a six-act drama: (1) the pre-Reformation scriptural meditation reform program; (2) an underground evangelical movement in the 1520s and early 1530s; (3) an independent Church of England under Henry VIII from 1534 to 1547, where the pope is rejected but Protestant theology not fully embraced; (4) a fully Protestant church guided by Archbishop Thomas Cranmer under Edward VI (1547–1553); (5) the restoration of the Roman Catholic Church under Mary (1553–1558), resulting in martyrdom for many, including Cranmer; and (6) the restoration of Cranmer's Protestant church under Elizabeth (1558–1603) and its subsequent defense.

Medieval English Affective Tradition

The English Reformation was not the product of Henry VIII's desire to gain a new wife. Although the king played an essential role
in how it developed, the renewal movement which culminated
in the Protestant Church of England had actually begun almost
two hundred years earlier. In fact, the roots go all the way back to
a curious, self-appointed hermit named Richard Rolle (d. 1349).
Despairing of the dry, academic theology he found as a student at
Oxford, Rolle quickly returned home, borrowed two tunics from his
sister, fashioned a makeshift hermit's outfit, and devoted himself to
a solitary life of spiritual contemplation. He believed passionately
that if those in religious orders would constantly meditate on Scripture, their hearts would eventually burn physically with an intense
love for God. This divinely given ardor would then lead them to
renounce the world and so find their greatest joy in God alone. For
Rolle, it was quite clear that the only way Christians could break
free from the supernatural power of sin and Satan was the even
greater supernatural power of God's Word, which alone would nur-
ture this all-conquering love for God in their hearts. Since Rolle
saw Scripture as the divine channel for spiritual power, he placed
special emphasis on the name of Jesus as the sum of the gospel message. If Christians would focus on the Holy Name, the word *Jesus*
being simple to keep on their lips and in their hearts, they would
experience transforming power in their lives.

> If you wish to be on good terms with God, and have his grace
> direct your life, and come to the joy of love, then fix this name
> "Jesus" so firmly in your heart that it never leaves your thought.
> And when you speak to him using your customary name "Jesu,"[1]
> in your ear it will be joy, in your mouth honey, and in your heart
> melody, because it will seem joy to you to hear that name being
> pronounced, sweetness to speak it, cheer and singing to think

[1]. *Iesu* is the correct Latin form for "Jesus" when said directly to him; consequently, in the
Middle Ages using *Jesu* in English prayers was common as a form of intimacy.

it. If you think of the name "Jesus" continually and cling to it devotedly, then it will cleanse you from sin and set your heart aflame; it will enlighten your soul, remove turbulence and eliminate lethargy; it will give the wound of love and fill the soul to overflowing with love; it will chase off the devil and eliminate terror, open heaven and create a mystic.[2]

A born evangelist for this mystical way of life, Rolle wrote extensively for those religious living in enclosed walls, in Latin (for men) and English (for women). Yet, shortly after his death, Rolle's writings began to circulate beyond just dedicated contemplatives to those who had worldly responsibilities but still wanted to maintain regular private devotions. Called the "mixed life tradition," this movement began as a call from Gregory the Great (c. 540–604) for clergy to support their life out in the community serving their people with a regular pattern of retreat from the world to pursue divine intimacy through prayer and meditation. Under the influence of Rolle's teaching, clerics in his native Yorkshire sought to maintain this balanced life of service and devotion. Because his writings were also widely available in the vernacular, some laypeople began to seek to follow the example of their spiritual advisors and use his work as devotional aids for their own pursuit of a mixed life.

By the 1380s, Walter Hilton (c. 1343–1396) was consciously adapting Rolle's literary legacy for such laity. Trained as a canon lawyer, most likely in Cambridge, Hilton eventually joined an Augustinian priory in the diocese of York, where he remained until his death. Whereas Rolle had been a man of extremes, an unabashed advocate for the superiority of a life dedicated exclusively to celibate contemplation and the sweet joys of the physical manifestations of burning love and melodic song that would follow, Hilton counseled moderation. In his *Epistle on Mixed Life*, he discouraged a lay lord who was considering renouncing his position and possessions in order to enter a religious order. While praising the lord's

---

2. Rosamund S. Allen, ed., *Richard Rolle: The English Writings* (New York: Paulist, 1988), 173.

intention, Hilton warned that he needed to temper his enthusiasm by taking a hard look at his position, for if his love for God was not disciplined, he could easily make bad judgments.[3] Citing the teaching of Gregory, Hilton advised his correspondent that to truly practice godly love, he should stay in his station, fulfilling his social obligations to serve his dependents while pursuing privately a life of devotion. After all, Jesus himself practiced a life of service to others punctuated by periodic withdrawal for private contemplation.[4]

With his characteristic concern for moderation, Hilton also advised the lay lord to concentrate on a loving devotion that would lead to moral reformation, rather than Rolle's physical manifestations:

Saint Augustine says that *the life of every good Christian man is a continual desire to God,* and such desire is great power and virtue.... And what is this desire? Surely it is nothing but a loathing of all this worldly bliss, a forsaking of all fleshly or sensual love in your heart, and an extreme loving, with a most hungry longing and thirsting after God.... Seek and nourish only this, and seek not after any feeling in thy corporal senses, external or internal, nor any sensible sweetness or devotion, neither by the ear nor by the taste of your palate, nor by any wonderful light or sight of your eyes, nor seek the sight of Angels, no, though our Lord Himself would appear in His body to the sight of your eyes, make no great matter of that; and therefore let all your diligence be that you may truly and really perceive and find in your soul, and especially in your will, a loathing and full forsaking of all manner of sin and all manner of uncleanness, with a spiritual seeing or perceiving how foul, how ugly and how painful these things be; and that you may have within you a mighty desiring of virtues, and, namely, of humility and charity, and finally, of the bliss of Heaven.[5]

---

3. Walter Hilton, *Epistle on Mixed Life,* chap. 1, in *The Scale (Or Ladder) of Perfection,* ed. J. B. Dalgairns (Westminster: Art and Book, 1908), 319.

4. Ibid., chap. 4, pp. 323–24.

5. Ibid., chap. 8, pp. 337–38 (the English has been modernized).

Hilton's masterwork, *The Scale of Perfection* (i.e., ladder to perfection), made that transformation in desire the hallmark of a life spent in regular meditation on Scripture. Of course, the use of the Holy Name of Jesus had a special role in this process: "I shall tell one word for all in the which you shall seek, desire, and find it, for in that one word is all that you have lost. This word is Jesu."[6] With devotion to the Holy Name a person's human desire for God would be "turned into love and affection, spiritual savor, and sweetness, into light and knowing of steadfastness."[7]

About the same time that Hilton was urging the laypeople of York to lead holy lives through practicing scriptural contemplation within the medieval church structure, John Wycliffe, a lecturer of theology at Oxford, went much further. Although he too wanted laypeople to commit themselves to leading godly lives, Wycliffe thought the key was rejecting the medieval church's very foundation, namely, the clergy's traditional role as the middlemen between God and his people. Deeply disillusioned by the worldly wealth and power the bishops and great monasteries had acquired in English society, Wycliffe rejected the institutional church of his day as hopelessly corrupt. Turning to the Scriptures as the sole authority for all knowledge instead, he rejected the church's monopoly on salvation. Confession to a priest was not necessary for the forgiveness of sins. Rather, Christians stood directly accountable to God for their actions. Since purgatory had no biblical foundation, indulgences were merely a clerical con game.

Since everyone needed to know the truth about how to live so as to please God, Wycliffe wanted laypeople to have the Bible in English so they could understand for themselves. Because of such teachings, he was eventually banished from Oxford and, some years after his death, officially declared a heretic by the Council of Basil (1415). However, his ideas did not die with him. Despite

---

6. Walter Hilton, *Scala Perfeccionis* (Westminster: Wynkyn de Worde, 1494), 1.46, E3r (the English has been modernized).

7. Ibid., E3v.

persecution, a small group called the Lollards continued to propagate his teachings underground in England up until the Reformation. Since the vernacular Scriptures were essential to Lollardy, in 1408 Thomas Arundel, archbishop of Canterbury, tried to suppress the heretical movement by permanently banning laypeople from having a copy of the Scriptures in English without a special license from their bishop.

Fifteenth-Century English Lay Piety

As part of its fight against Lollardy, the medieval English church encouraged two approved channels for the rising tide of lay devotion in the fifteenth century—one external, one internal. The illiterate were still encouraged to look to external images, rituals, and activities to fire their love for God. That is why medieval church interiors were filled with paintings of Bible stories, statues of saints illuminated by candles, and numerous reminders of Christ's death such as crucifixes, pietàs, and emblems of his passion. During the incense-filled Latin mass, the simple folk were to meditate on one of the holy images in the church, or repeat a devotion like the rosary, while waiting for the special moment to kneel and adore the elevated host with the rest of the congregation. During different church festivals such as Palm Sunday, Rogation Days, and Corpus Christi, they were to process around the parish. For acts of special devotion, they were to go on pilgrimages to holy places like the shrine of the Holy Family at Walsingham or the tomb of Saint Thomas à Becket at Canterbury. Finally, at least once a year during Holy Week they were to confess their sins to a priest so that they might receive absolution and be fit to partake of the consecrated bread during the Easter mass. All these various religious activities were designed to provide external stimuli appealing to the full gamut of the human senses—sight, smell, sound, touch, and taste—which would reach the inner soul of a Christian so as to stir up devotion.

Yet, relying on the physical senses was only the first step in spiritual development. For literate laypeople, the late-medieval English church turned to the writings of the English mystics to encourage a second, more advanced means of nurturing love for God and godliness. Rolle was without doubt the most popular English devotional writer of the fifteenth century, if the sheer abundance of over 450 surviving manuscripts is any indication. Hilton's work was also widely popular throughout the century. Cecily, Duchess of York, Edward IV's mother, had the *Epistle on Mixed Life* as one of the texts read to her during lunch. That great stalwart of the Lancasterian cause Lady Margaret Beaufort, Henry VII's mother, was equally devoted. The first printed texts of *The Scale of Perfection* and the *Epistle on Mixed Life* were published together in 1494 by the expressed "command" of that "mighty princess" Lady Margaret. Not surprisingly, then, the first edition selected the manuscript tradition that included a lengthy discussion of the name of Jesus. For in the same year as the printed text appeared, the pope appointed Lady Margaret patron of the Mass of the Holy Name in England. A true follower of this spiritual tradition, she was also well known for giving members of her household gold collars inscribed with hearts alternating with *IHS* (a partially Latinized version of the first three letters of *Jesus* in Greek)[8] as marks of her favor. Two generations later, Tudor royal wives were still relying on such conduits of supernatural power, perhaps for fertility. Both Catherine of Aragon and Jane Seymour had their portraits done with an *IHS* brooch upon their bosom.

The Tudors promoted Hilton's mixed life tradition because it fulfilled an essential part of their plan for renewing English society after the Wars of the Roses (1455–1485). The bitter blood feud between the rival families of Lancaster (the Red Rose) and York (the White Rose) had only proved too well the old African proverb that when elephants fight, the grass suffers. According to medieval ethics, the root cause of the conflict had been moral failure; the Yorkists had twice forsaken their duty in order to gain the throne. First, Edward IV had rebelled against his lord, Henry VI. Then,

---

8. I.e., the capital Greek iota and eta, but a capital Latin *S* rather than a Greek sigma.

Richard III had failed to protect the boy king Edward V and his brother—Richard's own nephews—despite his sworn oath to do so. The moral outrage of some of the English nobility at Richard's betrayal contributed greatly to Henry's ability to raise an army to defeat him at Bosworth Field in 1485. Consequently, the Tudors realized that civil peace in a feudal society did not depend upon a stable royal dynasty alone. Individuals had to be committed to fulfilling their duties in the social hierarchy as well. Inferiors needed to be obedient to their superiors, and superiors had to guard the best interests of their inferiors. In short, the foundation of all medieval order was personal morality, and the role of religion was to be its guardian, cultivating virtue and suppressing vice in society. Nothing, then, could be more helpful to the Tudor political agenda than the emphasis of the mixed life tradition on a Scripture-based affective piety leading to doing one's duty to God and neighbor.

Erasmus

For that very reason, the Tudors also became great supporters of Erasmian humanism. One could hardly find a greater proponent of either the mixed life tradition or the importance of moving the affections to ensure godly behavior than the great Dutch scholar Erasmus. On the one hand, his *Handbook for the Christian Life* (often referred to by its Latin title, the *Enchiridion*) was an international best seller advocating the practice of daily scriptural meditation to defend the soul against all spiritual assaults associated with an active life in worldly affairs. On the other hand, his rejection of scholasticism and many of the external medieval cultic practices was but the bitter fruit of his deeply rooted conviction that they had failed to touch the hearts of the people sufficiently to inspire them to love God and do good.

Erasmus delighted in contrasting the ridiculousness of scholastic subtleties to the absolute necessity of biblical morality: "I do not think that any man will count himself a faithful Christian because he can dispute with craft and tedious perplexity about the nature of words or things or ideas, but in that he acknowledges and expresses in deeds those things which Christ both taught and accomplished."[9] Erasmus wanted a church whose people would "not differ only in title and certain ceremonies from the heathen and unfaithful, but rather in the pure manner of our life." He mocked those who relied on external things to make them holy. He insisted that all people, from the highest in the land to the lowest, should immerse themselves in Scripture instead.[10] For Jesus spiritually indwelt its message: "The Gospel represents and expresses the living image of his most holy mind, indeed, Christ himself speaking, healing, dying, raising again and, to conclude, all parts of him."[11]

Erasmus was convinced that, once sowed in the heart, Scripture would move the people to love God and do good. Consequently, he used the same kind of highly affective language we have seen in Rolle and Hilton to urge Christians to devote themselves passionately to the Word of God: "Let us, therefore, all with fervent desire thirst after these spiritual springs. Let us embrace them. Let us be studiously conversant with them. Let us kiss these sweet words of Christ with a pure affection. Let us be newly transformed into them, for what we study shapes how we live."[12] Erasmus was quite clear that he did not want devotion to Scripture restricted to a spiritual elite consisting of celibates vowed to the church and wealthy laypeople. He urged making vernacular texts available to all, even the common, unlearned married person. For how else could the church and society really improve? To that end, Erasmus famously called for the ploughman at his plough and the weaver at his loom to sing biblical texts as they worked.

The merging of medieval English affective piety with Erasmus's sophisticated learning proved a powerful combination in Tudor England. Supported by Lady Margaret Beaufort and her circle, a

---

9. Erasmus, *An Exhortation to the Diligent Studye of Scripture* (Antwerp: Hoochstraten, 1529), A2 (the English has been modernized for all quotations from this text).

10. Ibid., [8]r.

11. Ibid., A6r.

12. Ibid., A5v.

whole group of scholars arose that urged an emphasis on the power of Scripture to move Christians to love God more than sin. These Tudor humanists were convinced that the new educational programs instituted at the universities would lead to better preachers, who would inspire better church communities, which would then eventually bring about a better English society. Cambridge particularly benefited from royal patronage since its chancellor, Bishop John Fisher, was the confessor and spiritual advisor to Lady Margaret. Jesus College, Christ's College, and St John's College were all founded as part of their efforts. Long before Luther, the leaders of English society were committed to a thorough reform and renewal of the medieval English church through an emphasis on the power of Scripture.

Having fully embraced Erasmian humanism as the antidote to both moral laxity among the orthodox and Lollardy among the heterodox, the Tudor establishment wanted nothing to do with a new heresy which would only impede their church-sanctioned reform efforts. When Luther's book attacking the sacraments, *The Babylonian Captivity of the Church*, led to his excommunication by the pope in 1521, Henry responded by gathering together Fisher and the other leading theologians from Oxford and Cambridge in April of the same year to help him write a defense of traditionalist teaching. Published in June, the result was the *Assertion of the Seven Sacraments*, for which the pope awarded Henry the title "Defender of the Faith." Reflecting Fisher's own inclusive humanist theology, the *Assertion* drew on the three-string cord of Scripture, the fathers, and the scholastics as mutually supportive of the medieval church's teachings. In his written responses, Luther showed a definite lack of deference, calling Henry, among other things, a "raging madman," "lying baboon," "wanton buffoon," "filth and vermin," "feminine," "foolish," "diseased," and one having a "blasphemous and malignant mouth."[13] The king never forgave Luther for such language, and never forgot.

---

13. Martin Luther, *Martin Luther against Henry VIII, King of England*, in *Luther's Controversial Tracts* (Dublin: Flynn, 1840), 1:5–7, 11–12.

England's First Evangelicals

Not all Tudor humanists, however, rejected Luther out of hand. Rolle and Hilton had taught them to look to the power of Scripture to transform their affections so that they could truly love God and godliness. Erasmus had reinforced that very message while calling for an *ad fontes* reform of much of medieval thought and practice, including the daring proposal to extend the teaching of vernacular biblical meditation to every ploughman. Luther's writings also called for a personal, inner connection between all Christians and their Savior through Scripture, even if he combined this approach to catholic renewal with a break from the traditionalist understanding of salvation far more radical than even Erasmus had suggested. For despite his rejection of the medieval emphasis on externals, Erasmus still had insisted that right conduct was necessary to win salvation. Scripture was the source both for knowing what a person had to do and for imparting to the person the power to do so, if one chose to respond. Since salvation depended on a person's ongoing set of choices, no one could be sure whether he or she would live well enough in the end to be saved. Luther, however, argued that Scripture had a very different role in salvation. Rather than being the means to try to become worthy of salvation, true meditation on Scripture, Luther argued, would only make individuals realize their complete inability to do so, leading to a sense of terror. However, the apostolic teaching of Paul made clear that salvation was a free gift that people received by faith, not by human accomplishments. When people dwelled on the promises of Scripture, God would send them the gift of faith that would, in an instant, unite them to him forever. This assurance, in turn, would free them from all fear and ignite in them instead a grateful love for God and neighbor.

In 1521 Luther's great colleague Philip Melanchthon explained this process in his groundbreaking *Loci Communes* ("Fundamental Theological Doctrines"). According to Melanchthon, what the heart loves, the will chooses and the mind justifies. Hence, after the fall of humanity, both human reason and human willpower are held captive by the affection of self-love, or concupiscence. As a result, on its own, the human heart naturally loves itself more than God and other people. The will chooses those things that make it feel good, and the mind rationalizes what has been done. The only way out of this closed circle of sin and selfishness is by "introducing better affections into souls."[14] Humanity has to discover a new, stronger ruling love—a love for God instead of a love for self.

But where does this stronger love for God come from? Guilt, fear, shame, duty, pride? That was the answer from the medieval Catholic church. According to Melanchthon, however, Scripture, teaches otherwise. When the good news of justification by faith is proclaimed, the Spirit assures Christians of their salvation by working supernaturally through the promises of God's Word. This new confidence in God's gracious goodwill toward them will re-orient the affections of believers, calming their turbulent hearts and inflaming in them a grateful love in return. In short, only the unconditional love of God made known in free salvation can birth a selfless love for God and others in the human heart. In the light of their own training in the importance of Scripture-stirred affections, some Tudor humanists found this argument thoroughly convincing, despite the opposition of the king and the church.

As a Cambridge lecturer, Thomas Bilney (c. 1495–1531) was one of the early leaders of this new kind of Tudor humanism. Ever the evangelist, he was responsible for many conversions, including Hugh Latimer, the famous preacher and martyr. His own conversion came unexpectedly through reading Erasmus's new Latin translation of the Bible. As a student of humanism, he had picked up the translation because of its reputation for eloquence rather than any interest in theology. As he read, however, he was struck by the promise that Jesus came into the world to save sinners. The one sentence of 1 Timothy 1:15 drove out all the desperation tormenting his heart, leaving him with a deep sense of inner peace instead. Ac-

---

14. D. Drews and D. Cohrs, eds., *Supplementa Melanchtoniana*, 5 vols. (Leipzig: Verein für Reformations-geschichte, 1910–1929), 2:33.

cording to Bilney, "After this, the Scripture began to be more pleasant to me than honey" because there "I learned that all my travails
[in penitential works]" were "a hasty and swift running out of the
right way" but that sinners could "obtain quietness and rest" when
"they believed in the promise of God."[15]

Bilney compared this experience to the story of the chronically
ill woman in Luke 8:43–48. She had spent twelve years seeking a
remedy for her ongoing bleeding, without success. Yet when she
managed in faith to touch the hem of Jesus's garment, "she was
so healed that immediately, she felt it in her body."[16] Note that she
"felt" her healing, and she felt it "immediately." Both points were
important to Bilney. At last, forgiveness had come to him in an instant rather than as the end result of a long and uncertain process.
Moreover, this forgiveness was experiential, not just cognitive.
The full pardon that justification by faith offered brought about an
instant transformation of his emotions, which he could feel deep
within him. Bilney's heart went from despair to joy. In modern par-
lance, his reading of Erasmus's New Testament had led to a classic
"born-again" Christian experience. Here was the motivation for his
love of evangelism. He sought to share with others the same pastoral strategy for inner affective wholeness that he himself had found
through justification by faith.

William Tyndale (c. 1494–1536) was another Tudor humanist
who eventually embraced the evangelical "new learning." While
a tutor to the family of Sir John Walsh in the west of England, he
translated the *Enchiridion* as an explanation for why he argued
with the local clergy who called at their home. Shortly afterward
in 1523, he went to London to seek the support of Bishop Tunstall
so he could fulfill the Erasmian ideal of translating the Bible into
English. Although Tunstall was a noted humanist highly praised by
Erasmus himself, he had absolutely no interest in such a project.
Disillusioned, Tyndale realized that he would have to carry out his

---

15. John Foxe, *Actes and Monuments* (London: John Day, 1570), 1141–43.
16. Ibid., 1141–42.

project beyond the reach of the English authorities. With the support of London merchants, he left for Germany in 1524. By 1526 Tyndale had produced the first English New Testament, copies of which were promptly smuggled into the ports of England in bales of cloth. Tunstall just as quickly banned them and organized a book burning at St Paul's Cathedral in London to reinforce his public opposition to the Scriptures in English.

While on the continent, Tyndale openly embraced the evangelical faith. Although he has left us no written account of his own conversion, his writings show that he, too, saw justification by faith as the way to transform the human affections from fear to love:

> In believing the heart is saved from the fear of everlasting death, and made sure of everlasting life; and then being overcome with this kindness, begins to love again and to submit itself unto the laws of God, to learn them and to walk in them. Note now the order: first God gives me light to see the goodness and righteousness of the law, and my own sin and unrighteousness; out of which knowledge springs repentance.... Then the same Spirit works in mine heart trust and confidence, to believe the mercy of God and his truth, that he will do as he hath promised; which belief saves me. And immediately out of that trust springs love toward the law of God again.[17]

Like Rolle, Hilton, and Erasmus before him, Tyndale insisted that believers actually experienced their connection to God. When an opponent demanded to know how he knew that he was saved, Tyndale responded that believers know and feel that it is true because the Holy Spirit has written the conviction on their hearts through Scripture. He used the analogy that just as there is a marked difference between children being told that a candle will burn their fingers and their actually touching the flames to experience the reality for themselves, so saving faith brings about

---

17. Henry Walter, ed., *An Answer to Sir Thomas More's Dialogue, The Supper of the Lord . . . and William Tracy's Testament Expounded by William Tyndale* (Cambridge: Parker Society, 1850), 195–96 (the English has been modernized for all quotations from this text).

a perceptible change in the affections of the heart. In short, early English evangelicals like Tyndale and Bilney adopted justification by faith to finally experience the kind of affective relationship with God that their teachers had demanded as the authentic hallmark of true Christianity.

If some English scholars began to embrace Luther's new teachings as the means of fulfilling the goals of Lady Margaret's humanist education reforms, the government and church were having none of it. Both Bilney and Tyndale were given a martyr's fiery crown. Yet, Tyndale's last words were reported to be a prayer for Henry VIII: "Lord, open the king of England's eyes." For, indeed, the best hope for the rapid spread of the evangelical faith in England was for Henry to change his mind and endorse a vernacular Bible and justification by faith. Such an about-face seemed highly unlikely for the newly minted "Defender of the Faith"—that is, until his marital difficulties found the king questioning the pope's trustworthiness as a reliable guide to the will of God. While Henry's "divorce" was not the beginning of the English Reformation, it dramatically changed the circumstances for its advancement.

Henry's "Divorce"

When Henry VII died in 1509, all English hopes for continued stability and prosperity rested on Henry VIII, the sole surviving male heir of his father. As a new seventeen-year-old king, Henry was persuaded to maintain England's political alliance with Spain by marrying Catherine of Aragon, the Spanish princess who was the widow of his older brother, Arthur, dead now seven years. Since Leviticus 18:16 specifically forbids a man from sleeping with his sister-in-law, Pope Julius II used papal authority to grant a dispensation permitting the marriage to proceed. Although their marriage gave every appearance of being a happy union for almost two decades, Catherine was never able to give Henry a son and heir to the throne. Of her six pregnancies, the first son, named Henry after his father, lived only long enough for incredibly elaborate celebrations of royal happiness to take place. With heartbreaking pathos, soon after the festivities in the young prince's honor drew to a close, so did his life of a mere fifty-two days. The next two pregnancies were sons as well, but stillborn. Only Mary, born in 1516, survived. It was unclear in those days whether she, as a female, could inherit the crown. After all, the only previous attempt by a woman to ascend the English throne had occurred over 350 years before and had merely led to nearly twenty years of civil war known as the Anarchy. Well aware of the consequences for his country if he did not leave behind a clear successor, Henry was determined to maintain his father's great accomplishment of restoring political stability to the land.

As it became obvious that Catherine was no longer of childbearing age, the words of Leviticus 20:21 began to haunt the king, for the verse declared a curse of childlessness on a marriage such as his. Indeed, some scholars of the day even suggested that the Hebrew text could mean "without heir," Henry's exact situation. Of course, Deuteronomy 25:5 also commands a man to marry his brother's widow if the brother has died without a son (as was the case with Arthur), so as to raise up an heir to the dead brother through the new marriage. Henry and his scholars, however, argued that the injunction from Deuteronomy was merely part of the civil and ceremonial law of ancient Israel, rules designed specially for the Jewish people at that time and no longer applicable after the coming of Christ. The Levitical prohibition, however, was part of the universal moral law, like the Ten Commandments—binding on all people for all time. Yet, in his own mind, Henry needed no further proof that his marriage violated divine law than the deaths of his three sons.

Convinced that his marriage to Catherine was invalid, he decided to marry the woman with whom he had now fallen in love, Anne Boleyn. In 1527, the king turned to Pope Clement VII for an annulment on the grounds of entering into a marriage contrary to Scripture. Cardinal Wolsey, Henry's top advisor at the time, suggested that the pope might be more open to granting such a request if the king argued that the lawyers had made an error in drawing up the document granting permission. Naturally, it was easier for Clement to blame shoddy legal paperwork for the annulment than to admit that Julius II had lacked the authority to grant permission for the wedding in the first place. Despite such shrewd counsel, Henry took the harder road. Believing that he was under divine punishment, he insisted that Clement admit his sin and allow him to repent by entering into a new marriage approved by God.

The pope had no desire to offend either Henry or Catherine's very powerful nephew, Emperor Charles V, whose troops had sacked Rome only a few months earlier. Consequently, Clement VII simply delayed in rendering any decision. Even though he allowed Wolsey to convene a hearing for a decision on Henry's petition at the London home of the Dominican Blackfriars in 1529, in the end the case was still appealed to Rome, where it languished. Exasperated, the king forced Wolsey to retire in disgrace and began a campaign against papal authority in England. Eventually, two men came to the fore in this effort, Thomas Cromwell and Thomas Cranmer.

A former senior advisor to Wolsey, Cromwell (c. 1485–1540) was gifted in political strategy and organizational efficiency. He had had a hard upbringing under an alcoholic father of moderate means. Leaving home as a teenager, he went to Europe to fight as a foot soldier for the French in Italy. He eventually left the army and made his way in the world of Continental commerce, first attaching himself to the household of an Italian merchant banker and then becoming a cloth dealer in the Netherlands. By the 1520s he had made a name for himself in commercial and legal circles in London, which led to his employment by Wolsey. A hardened survivor, Cromwell had both the radical vision and the ruthless tenacity necessary to find a legal way to solve the king's marital problem. Although he remained utterly loyal to Wolsey, both men realized that the best way Cromwell could help his former boss was to gain the king's confidence. It did not take Cromwell long. Within a year he was working for the king. Six months later he became a member of the council. Soon he was directing building works for the king and devising the royal legislative strategy for Parliament. By 1533, Cromwell was Henry's top advisor. He devised the plan that ultimately freed Henry from his first marriage.

Thomas Cranmer (1489–1556)

Cranmer was a cautious, deliberate thinker who felt deeply but disciplined his responses thoroughly. As he gradually came to realize the indisputable power of God's unconditional love made known through Scripture, he became determined to rework the teachings of the Church of England accordingly. Born into a very modest but still genteel English family in Nottinghamshire, he was baptized into the traditional faith of the medieval church. Educated locally until he was fourteen, he went up to Jesus College, Cambridge, where he devoted himself to the study of theology. Eventually, he became a doctor of divinity in 1526. Along the way, Cranmer married, but within the year he was again single, having lost both his wife and their child during birth. Shortly thereafter, Cranmer committed himself to the priesthood with its traditional vow of celibacy.

Deeply influenced by Erasmus, Cranmer insisted that his Cambridge students base their theology primarily on the plain sense of Scripture rather than the church's own authority. When Henry's "divorce" made that an issue of national significance after the debacle at Blackfriars, the king invited Cranmer to join his team of scholars in 1529. Three years later, Henry VIII sent Cranmer to the continent on a diplomatic mission to try to win the support of Emperor Charles V. While in Germany, Cranmer encountered firsthand the new teachings of Martin Luther, the Wittenberg University professor, and his fellow Protestants. Up until this time, Cranmer had continued to believe, like Erasmus, that people had to do their best to become worthy of God's approval. Now Cranmer made a bold decision that determined the remainder of his life. He adopted the Lutheran understanding that only the unconditional love of God made known in justification by faith saved sinners. And, like Luther, who was a married former monk, Cranmer also decided clerical celibacy was unscriptural. Sealing his new commitment to the Protestant cause, he married again, this time to Margaret, a close relative of the German Reformer Andreas Osiander.

What makes a man in middle age turn his back on lifelong beliefs to stand alongside those he had previously argued were heretics? Not surprisingly, divine love was once again at the root. Although Cranmer left us no written account of what led to his new convictions, we can gain some insight from his programmatic Renaissance portrait from 1545. In the Gerlach Flicke painting, now found today in London's National Portrait Gallery, the Primate of All England is depicted seated, holding a copy of Saint Paul's Epistles in his hands, while a copy of Saint Augustine's *On Faith and Works* lies on a table in front of him. Although Cranmer always considered Scripture the ultimate theological authority, the Flicke portrait helps us understand the process by which Cranmer came to reject the medieval interpretation of Saint Paul.

Cranmer began by reading Augustine's definitive work on faith and good works, which taught something very different from the scholastic theologians. On the one hand, Augustine clearly stated that Paul's teaching on justification by faith meant that good works did not precede justification but followed it. Why? Because only works done out of love for righteousness could be considered good, and such love only came from the Holy Spirit. How, then, could someone seek to perform "good works" in order to gain the Holy Spirit? It was impossible. The whole medieval understanding of salvation was unbiblical, and the writings of Augustine—probably the most influential theologian of the Western church—supported such a conclusion. On the other hand, Augustine argued that once the Holy Spirit had united believers to Christ, their living faith necessarily brought about a deep, abiding love to honor God by performing good works. That's why Paul urged the churches to seek to lead a godly life of service just as Christ did.

Augustine's contention that Christian faith always manifested

itself in works of service deeply undercut the claim of traditionalists that people who thought they were saved by grace alone would
live just to please themselves. As Paul wrote in Romans 5:1–5, peace
with God through faith led to a heart filled with love, and this divine love transformed a believer's way of life. Here was the biblical
basis for the Protestant understanding of how justification by faith
produced a godly life. Love would lead the way, and that love would
only arise in believers' hearts once they realized God would give
them an unmerited, permanent peace with him by merely trusting
his promises.

Consequently, for Cranmer, unconditional love was the hallmark of true Christianity. He was famous for not holding a grudge
against his many enemies, no matter how close they came to bringing about his destruction. Indeed, Cranmer was notorious for not
only pardoning those who conspired against him but even going so
far as to do his best to advance their personal interests after they
apologized at least a little. As William Shakespeare had Henry VIII
put it,

> Do my Lord of Canterbury
> a shrewd turn, and he is your friend for ever.[18]

To Bishop Stephen Gardiner, Cranmer's principal theological
opponent, Cranmer's easy forgiveness of his enemies was, as Shakespeare once again aptly expressed it, but "words and weakness."[19]
When chided about this trait, Cranmer responded:

> What will you have a man do to someone that is not yet come to
> the knowledge of the truth of the Gospel . . . ? Shall we perhaps,
> in his journey coming towards us, by severity and cruel behavior
> overthrow him, and as it were in his pilgrimage stop him? I do
> not take this to be the way to allure men to embrace the doctrine
> of the Gospel. And if it be a true rule of our Savior Christ to do

---

18. William Shakespeare, *Henry VIII*, act 5, scene 3, lines 176–77.
19. Ibid., line 72.

good for evil, then let such as are not yet come to favor our religion learn to follow the doctrine of the Gospel by our example in using them in a friendly and charitable manner.[20]

To Cranmer, therefore, nothing helped his contemporaries better understand Protestant teaching than this evangelism of loving the unworthy. Since God loved sinners enough to save and bless them despite their lack of personal merit, Cranmer characteristically did likewise. This emphasis on God's love for the unworthy would be the common thread that ran throughout Cranmer's subsequent theological writings.

Since he had now committed himself to the Protestant understanding of salvation, nothing could have been more unexpected and unwelcome for Cranmer than Henry VIII's surprising call for him to return to England to become the new archbishop of Canterbury. The king had no idea that Cranmer was no longer an Erasmian humanist but actually an evangelical one. Very slow to make his journey back, Cranmer eventually agreed to the new post. No doubt he became convinced that it was his God-given duty to help the Church of England become Protestant, just as he himself had. To be successful, however, he would have to persuade Henry to become supportive of the new teachings, for only a king had the power to reform his country's church when the pope would not. Henry's willingness to renounce the Roman pontiff made him the best hope of evangelical clergy like Cranmer.

The Independent Church of England under Henry VIII

When Cranmer arrived back in England in January 1533, he squared his shoulders with characteristic discipline and began the truly formidable task of trying to implement the principles of the Continental Reformation in the English church. On Passion Sunday, March 30, 1533, Cranmer was consecrated the sixty-ninth archbishop of

---

20. John Gough Nichols, ed., *Narratives of the Days of the Reformation*, first series, 77 (London: Camden Society, 1859), 246–47 (the English has been modernized in this text).

Canterbury. Since the service included oaths of allegiance to the pope, Cranmer swore a solemn protestation beforehand, declaring that such oaths would not prevent him from following the law of God, his loyalty to the king, and his commitment to reform the English church.

The next month Cromwell pushed through Parliament the Act in Restraint of Appeals, which made the king, rather than the pope, the final legal authority in English ecclesiastical court cases. Now, with Henry's permission, Cranmer convened a court to issue a final ruling on the king's "great matter." On May 23 he annulled Henry's marriage to Catherine as contrary to Scripture. Since Henry and Anne had secretly wed the previous January, Cranmer crowned her Queen of England on June 1, 1533. The following year, Parliament declared that the king and his heirs were, by divine right, the supreme head on earth of the Church of England. With the Act of Royal Supremacy, the English church was now fully independent of Rome.

Loosed from papal authority, the English church began a patchy process of reform. Like Erasmus, Henry held that Scripture had the authority to reject certain medieval church teachings and traditions. All doctrine and ceremonies in the Church of England henceforth had to be proved by the Word of God, as interpreted in the light of the early church by governmental authority. For convinced evangelicals like Cranmer, royal supremacy and the new emphasis on Scripture offered the best hope for bringing the truths of the Reformation to the English people. For the archbishop's traditionalist opponents, the king's new-found authority and loathing of Luther remained the best means of preventing any further alterations in faith and practice. In general, Cromwell supported Protestant-oriented reform, doing the hard political work to advance proposals sympathetic to Cranmer's agenda. Henry, however, remained more circumspect. He supported changes broadly in line with Erasmian humanism but would not tolerate Protestant doctrine on salvation or the mass.

For the rest of the 1530s, the evangelical cause gradually made headway against traditional medieval religion. In 1535, Henry delegated his authority over the Church of England to Cromwell as his "vice-gerent in spirituals." As a result, Cromwell now outranked Cranmer in ecclesiastical matters. With his new authority, Cromwell began the campaign against the monasteries of England and Wales in 1536. Four years later, all religious orders had been disbanded and their property seized by the state. No doubt the king and his courtiers were eager to enrich themselves with the vast acres of monastic land. Yet, for Cromwell and Henry, practical political concerns were also surely involved. Anyone who took possession of former church property, no matter how small, was automatically excommunicated from the Roman Catholic Church. Consequently, the distribution of monastic lands literally bought support for Henry's church from among the most powerful in Tudor society. That Henry turned a blind eye to local people helping themselves to small items from his monastic properties as well only expanded the incrimination to the common people. Equally important, however, the monasteries were seen as hot spots for opposition to royal supremacy. The conservative religious uprisings in the north of England in 1536 only reinforced in Henry's mind the need to close the monasteries as a way to suppress rebellion.

Yet, even beyond these political reasons, the Henrician reformers had sound theological grounds for wanting to see them shut. Despite all of monasticism's many truly admirable contributions, both to the Christian faith and to human society in general, its whole premise was the spiritual superiority of this way of life. The vows of obedience, poverty, and celibacy set the members of religious orders above laypeople as holier people whose prayers were especially powerful. Yet, Erasmus had severely criticized most monastic communities as falling far short of such a high standard. On the one hand, he was scandalized by how often they simply went through the ceremonial motions of their prayers without any inner religious fervor or serious pursuit of personal holiness. On the other hand, too many monastic communities were willing to take advantage of gullible laypeople by promoting phony relics to lure the lucrative pilgrimage trade. Cromwell's agents made sure to spread stories about wildly flagrant examples of both sorts of failings, seeking to tar the whole movement with the misdeeds of some.

Yet, there was an even deeper theological issue. The whole point of both Erasmian humanism and Lutheran teaching was the breaking down of the spiritual hierarchy represented by monasticism. Both Erasmus and Luther wanted the married ploughman as much as the celibate monk to engage in affective scriptural meditation. Indeed, they both urged that the home, not the monastery, be considered the best place to transmit religious values. However, Luther went even one step further. He condemned monasticism as institutionalized works-righteousness, a way of life inherently contrary to the true nature of Paul's teaching on justification. Seen in this light, for evangelicals like Cranmer the Protestant gospel had no greater enemy in England than the cult of merit that was medieval monasticism.

Concerning doctrinal matters, Cromwell gathered together a group of both traditionalist and evangelical bishops in 1537 to draw up a set of standard sermons to be read in parishes. The result was the *Institution of a Christian Man*, popularly known as the Bishops' Book. An attempt at theology by committee, the resulting work was at best a patchwork compromise. Bishop Gardiner disparagingly compared the book to a barn where all parties were able to store up their favorite theological beliefs, while ignoring the rest.[21] Yet, to a gospel man like Cranmer, even this hodgepodge was a decided step forward, precisely because so much Protestant theology had at last made its way into official church teaching, regardless of the theological company it was required to keep there. When Henry VIII criticized the more Protestant sections of the Bishops' Book, Cranmer wrote back in 1538 seeking to reinforce the affective

---

21. James Arthur Muller, ed., *The Letters of Stephen Gardiner* (Cambridge: Cambridge University Press, 1933), 351.

evangelical principle that love for God and king was the spiritual fruit of justification by faith:

> But, if the profession of our faith of the remission of our own sins enter within us into the deepness of our hearts, then it must kindle a warm fire of love in our hearts towards God, and towards all other for the love of God,—a fervent mind to seek and procure God's honour, will, and pleasure in all things,—a good will and mind to help every man and to do good unto them, so far as our might, wisdom, learning, counsel, health, strength, and all other gifts which we have received of God, will extend,— and, in summary, firm intent and purpose to do all that is good, and leave all that is evil.[22]

The king, however, remained unconvinced. Not surprisingly, then, the Cromwell-inspired negotiations that summer between Henry and the ambassadors from the German Protestant military league on a proposed theological concordat ended in failure.

Nevertheless, Henry VIII did agree to the greatest, long-sought, joint Erasmian and evangelical goal. He permitted the lifting of the ban on vernacular Scriptures for England. In 1538, Cromwell ordered that every parish in the country set forth a large English Bible for public use. To enable them to do so, the royally commissioned Great Bible, based largely on the work of Tyndale, came off the printing presses in April 1539. Since Cranmer wrote a preface for later editions in which he outlined how Scripture was to be read, the book is sometimes referred to as Cranmer's Bible. With all these advances, little wonder Ralph Morice, Cranmer's principal secretary, called the period "this most happy world of godly reformation."[23] Sadly, it was not to last.

With characteristic abruptness, a month after the publication of the Great Bible, the king suddenly made clear that he had, for the moment, reached the limit of his Erasmian reforming tendencies. In

---

22. John E. Cox, ed., *Miscellaneous Writings and Letters of Thomas Cranmer* (Cambridge: Parker Society, 1846), 86 (the English is modernized in all quotations from this text).

23. Ralph Morice to Thomas Cromwell, *State Papers* 1/113, 208r.

May 1539, Henry endorsed the Act of Six Articles, which entrenched key conservative theological principles, among them transubstantiation and clerical celibacy. To add deep personal loss on top of a thorough public defeat, Cranmer now had to send his well-hidden wife abroad. Far worse, however, on July 28, 1540, Henry went so far as to behead Thomas Cromwell for, among other matters, supposedly supporting those who denied transubstantiation. Nothing could better convey that Henry's flirtation with Germany was over. Just in case the king's message had not been understood, two days later Henry had three Lutherans burned as heretics, including Robert Barnes, his former ambassador to the German Protestants. Seeking to be even-handed, however, the king had three papal loyalists hanged for treason against the royal supremacy as well.

Henry's ideal for the English church was clearly a commitment to Erasmian catholic principles, but without the pope. Consequently, in 1543 the king had his clergy draw up a new, consistently conservative doctrinal statement, *A Necessary Doctrine*. Popularly known as the King's Book, its sermons affirmed both transubstantiation and the necessity of works for salvation. Yet, in keeping with Erasmus's teaching and the king's own deep suspicion of priestly pretension to spiritual authority, the King's Book broke with medieval tradition, as well as the Bishops' Book, and denied the necessity of confession to a priest for salvation. Still, with justification by faith explicitly condemned by the King's Book, the conservatives on the king's council now felt confident enough to plot Cranmer's downfall. Only the dramatic last-minute personal intervention of Henry VIII saved the archbishop from going the way of Cromwell.

Nevertheless, within a few years, Henry unexpectedly changed course again. As his death approached, the king probably decided that his greatest accomplishment was England as a "pope-free zone," and he rightly surmised that only the evangelicals would maintain that legacy. In the end, he wrote his will so that Cranmer and his fellow believers were to guide his underage son after his death on January 28, 1547.

The Protestant Church of England

Thus, under the boy-king Edward VI (1537–1553), Cranmer was at last free to reshape the teaching and practices of the English church according to biblical truth. During the next six and a half short years, Cranmer worked hard to produce a new, Protestant blueprint for the Church of England. Since the mission of the church was to proclaim the message, the very first liturgical change Cranmer made under Edward was the publication of an official set of sermons called the Book of Homilies (1547). Required reading in every parish, the Homilies taught *sola Scriptura* and justification by faith. Next he brought out a progressively more Protestant Book of Common Prayer (1549 and 1552) to reinforce the message of the Homilies. The first prayer book insisted on English as the language of the liturgy, restored systematic reading of Scripture, and removed all references to both personal merit and the mass as a propitiatory sacrifice. The Ordinal (1550) grounded the role of deacons, priests, and bishops in New Testament practice. The revised, second Book of Common Prayer (1552) went even further than the first, making clear that Christ's eucharistic presence was spiritual in nature, a holy communion in the heart of the believer through personal faith.

With the new services of daily Morning and Evening Prayer, Cranmer had taken the very final step in the two-hundred-year process of completely laicizing monastic affective scriptural meditation. Since his Word-based services were fitted around the average person's work day, Cranmer had made it possible for the mixed life's tradition of biblical rumination to be the rhythmic daily norm for every English person, not just a special, holier, privileged few. Finally, in the last months of the boy-king's life, Cranmer drew up a concise official statement of doctrine called the Articles of Religion (1553). Summing up the theological beliefs that had shaped the message of the Edwardian church, the Forty-Two Articles applied Reformed scriptural exegesis to the controversial issues of the day, including justification, the sacraments, and predestination.

The Reign of Mary Tudor

Edward VI died on July 6, 1553. Although he had been a vigorous youth, even engaging in knightly tournaments, he contracted tuberculosis at age fifteen and died within six months. After a short-lived attempt by the boy-king and his advisors to maintain the Protestant advances by putting his cousin Lady Jane Grey on the throne, Edward was soon succeeded by his half-sister Mary, a devout Roman Catholic. During her brief reign, she married Philip II of Spain, and they jointly did their best to restore England to Roman Catholicism, including papal allegiance. Many evangelical activists fled to Protestant centers on the Continent, gaining firsthand experience of Reformed churches there. Nearly three hundred who stayed behind were burned as heretics, Cranmer himself being the chief example.

He was arrested in September 1553, soon after he denounced the return of the Latin mass as blasphemous. Two years later he was tried and found guilty of heresy for denying papal authority and transubstantiation. On October 16, he was forced to watch the burning of Hugh Latimer, the famous preacher, and Nicholas Ridley, bishop of London. The latter died horrifically, his legs slowly burned away, but his upper body remaining whole, leaving Ridley in screaming agony. The shock of such a sight, the academic doubts raised by the Spanish friars assigned to win him back to the papist faith, and the memory of the common evangelical practice under Henry of recanting today in order to live to fight another clearly began to take their toll. On January 28, 1556, Cranmer signed the first of what would become a famous series of increasingly more abject recantations of the Protestant beliefs he had dedicated his archiepiscopate to introducing into England. By the time he signed the final, groveling confession on March 18, 1556, Cranmer would have known he could do nothing to save his life. He was simply a broken man, looking to his captors for assurance of what he should believe.

On March 21, the morning of his death, Cranmer awoke to find that he had newfound strength and assurance to renounce his recantations. According to a contemporary account, having previously been distraught, Cranmer came to the stake with "a cheerful countenance and willing mind."

> Fire being now put to him, he stretched out his right Hand, and thrust it into the Flame, and held it there a good space, before the Fire came to any other Part of his Body; where his Hand was seen of every Man sensibly burning, crying with a loud Voice, *This Hand hath offended.* As soon as the Fire got up, he was very soon Dead, never stirring or crying all the while.[24]

His Catholic executioners surely thought Cranmer was making satisfaction to his Protestant God. Yet, his understanding of the nature of salvation would have taught him otherwise, for the God he served saved the unworthy. Because he was God's child, the burden of all the multitude of his sins was no cause for him to distrust or despair of help at his Father's hand. For the incredible richness of God's merciful love for him would never have shone brighter than on that cloudy day, precisely because he, the chief promoter of the new faith, had fallen so far as to become a declared enemy of the gospel.

In the eyes of his critics, Cranmer's recantations prove that, at best, he was weak and vacillating. In the hearts of his admirers, however, Cranmer's final renunciation proved his true commitment to the Protestant faith. To Cranmer, his hand in the fire would have been an act of loving service from a grateful heart turned back to God by the power and promise of his immeasurably loving grace. His firmness of purpose would have been sustained by the hope he expressed in the Burial Office that was never read for him: "The souls of them that be elected, after they be delivered from the burden of the flesh, be in joy and felicity."[25] In the end, Cranmer's heart did not burn. His Catholic opponents thought it a sign of the presence of poisonous

---

24. From the description of Cranmer's death by "J. A.," British Library Harley MS 422, fols. 48–52; reprinted in John Strype, *Memorials of . . . Thomas Cranmer, Sometime Lord Archbishop of Canterbury*, 2 vols. in 1 (London: Richard Chiswell, 1694), bk. 3, chap. 21, 1:389.

25. Joseph Ketley, ed., *The Two Liturgies . . . in the Reign of King Edward the Sixth* (Cambridge: Parker Society, 1844), 319.

heresy lurking within it. However, to those attuned to his affective scriptural piety, perhaps Cranmer had preached his final and best sermon—that as this life comes to an end, the only thing that will endure is the love in a heart transformed by the good news of the gospel.

The Elizabethan Church

Because of such burnings, Queen Mary I has gone down in history as "Bloody Mary." Yet, crucially, she drew the line at her Protestant-sympathizing half-sister, Elizabeth, the daughter of Anne Boleyn. Despite the advice of some of her Spanish advisors, Mary refused to let any harm come Elizabeth's way. Consequently, when Mary died childless in 1558, Elizabeth came to the throne. The new queen quickly restored the clearly Protestant ethos of Edward's reign. In 1559, Parliament declared Elizabeth to be supreme governor and reissued both the 1547 Book of Homilies and a slightly amended 1552 Book of Common Prayer. In 1563, the bishops also approved a new, second Book of Homilies, and the revision of the Forty-Two Articles into Thirty-Nine was concluded in 1571. Older Anglican scholarship has often described the minor changes between the Edwardian and Elizabethan formularies as representing a middle way (*via media*) between Rome and Geneva. For example, the 1549 words of administration in Holy Communion permitted a real presence understanding of the sacrament: "The Body of our Lord Jesus Christ which was broken for you, preserve your body and soul unto everlasting life." However, the 1552 words clearly emphasized commemoration: "Take and eat this in remembrance that Christ died for you and feed on him in your heart by faith with thanksgiving." Elizabeth's 1559 prayer book simply combined them, giving parishioners the option of which phrase to emphasize.

Yet, it would be wrong to read into these changes any accommodation toward Roman Catholicism. The sermons of the second Book of Homilies were read alongside the 1559 Book of Common Prayer in the vast majority of Elizabethan parishes, and they were stridently anti-Roman. Essential practices associated with "mum-mish massing" were clearly condemned, including "gay gazing" at the elevated host and "the blasphemous buying and selling the most precious Body and Blood of Christ."[26] Indeed, the "Homily for Repairing and Keeping Clean of Churches" even made the rather gratuitous argument that just as the national authorities had swept the churches free from the superstitious filthiness of Roman idolatry, so too the local people should keep their church interiors free from the natural filthiness of bird droppings.[27] Moreover, the Thirty-Nine Articles explicitly rejected essential Roman Catholic teaching on the mass by rejecting transubstantiation, gazing at the host, lay reception of the consecrated bread alone, and the priestly offering of Christ for the forgiveness of sin and for release from the punishments of purgatory. Instead, Article 29 affirms the Reformed position that the wicked do not receive Christ in the sacrament. Consequently, the current scholarly consensus agrees that the Elizabethan changes to the Edwardian formularies were actually intended to make for a more comprehensive Protestantism that would be less offensive to Lutherans. If the Elizabethan settlement was a *via media*, it was between Geneva and Wittenberg.

Naturally, Elizabeth's religious policy immediately required defense against Roman accusations of heresy. John Jewel's *Apology for the Church of England* (1562) used immense humanist learning to argue that the consensus of the fathers of the first six centuries proved that the innovator in religion was the Church of Rome, not the biblically faithful Church of England. Thirty years later, Richard Hooker (1554–1600) had to defend the Elizabethan Settlement against those who thought it not Protestant enough. Believing the Bible to contain a blueprint for all aspects of the Christian life, activist Puritans argued that only presbyterian order and a preaching-centered service were divinely instituted in the New Testament. To answer these charges, Hooker's *Laws of Ecclesiastical Polity* first

---

26. John Griffiths, ed., *Two Books of Homilies Appointed to Be Read in Churches* (Oxford: Oxford University Press, 1859), 442, 349, 277.

27. Ibid., 278.

carefully placed the traditional Anglican emphasis on Scripture, the fathers, and scholarship in a broader context of the means of God's self-revelation, both directly through Scripture and indirectly through creation and human reason. He then narrowed what Scripture directly addresses to the essential matter of Christian doctrine, leaving such nonessentials as church order and ceremonies to be determined by national authorities, as guided in specifics by any relevant biblical passages, human wisdom, and church tradition. Consequently, the English church had freedom to retain bishops and Cranmer's liturgy, since neither of these was contrary to Scripture. In this way, Hooker faithfully defended the basic theological principles of the Edwardian Reformation, but in a much more detailed and sophisticated manner.

Conclusion

Thus, the English Reformation was an almost three-hundred-year-long process, beginning with the first stirrings of an affective biblical piety with Richard Rolle, culminating in the Reformation formularies which introduced evangelical scriptural piety into the rhythms of everyday English life and then the defense and deepening of these theological principles by the Elizabethan apologists Jewel and Hooker.

At the very heart of this generous Protestantism was the power of Scripture, through its teaching of justification by faith, to impart saving trust and transforming love to the wayward hearts and wandering wills of sinners. For according to Reformation Anglicanism, the glory of God is to love the unworthy. In the remaining chapters of this book we will examine each of its four key doctrines: *sola Scriptura*, "by Scripture alone"; *sola fide*, "by faith alone"; *sola gratia*, "by grace alone"; and *soli Deo gloria*, "glory to God alone." These timeless truths still have the power today to win people from their own works to Christ and his cross, thereby releasing them to love and serve God and their neighbors. What better program could there be for a modern renewal of Anglicanism than a revival of its authentic Reformation heritage?

CHAPTER 3

Sola Scriptura

John W. Yates III

We live in a world awash with ink. High-quality books are available in thousands of languages and distributed to every corner of the globe. Where the printed word is unavailable or out of fashion, entire libraries can be accessed with the swipe of a finger. The Bible has never been more widely available. The complete text of Scripture can be found in nearly five hundred languages. Portions of Scripture have been translated into more than twenty-five hundred languages. Never before have so many people had such thorough access to Scripture.

The world has not always been this way. Through the turbulent early decades of the English Reformation, the public reading of God's Word in the common language of the people was, in fact, forbidden. The clerical elite closely guarded Scripture, and its Latin text was jealously protected. In the official dogma of the church, Scripture was difficult to understand and prone to misinterpretation. To make it available to the people was to risk a profusion of heresies and disorder.

For those in the English church pushing for reform, this was a risk they were willing to take. For them the popular Reformation slogan *sola Scriptura* was a cry of hope and a plea for change.

The Story Begins

On August 13, 1537, Thomas Cranmer, archbishop of Canterbury, finally received the news he longed for with great intensity. King Henry VIII had consented to the official publication of the Bible in the English language. God's word written was going to be available, and Cranmer's dream of a renewed church in England was one step closer to reality.

Upon hearing the news, Cranmer wrote to Thomas Cromwell, chief minister to the king, who had convinced the king of the decision and notified Cranmer of their victory. Cranmer wrote with undisguised excitement:

> You have showed me more pleasure herein, than if you had given me a thousand pound; I doubt not but that hereby such fruit of good knowledge shall ensue, that it shall well appear hereafter, what high and acceptable service you have done unto God and the king: which shall so redound to your honour, that, beside God's reward, you shall obtain perpetual memory for the same within this realm.[1]

With the king's decision, not only was the Bible now to be made available; it was also to be read in public. An injunction issued shortly thereafter (1538) required all parish churches to purchase and display a Bible in English. Clergy were instructed that "one book of the whole Bible of the largest volume in English" was to be "set up in some convenient place within the . . . church," where "parishioners may . . . read it." Clergy were forcefully told, "Ye shall discourage no man . . . from the reading or hearing of the said Bible." The all-important first step for the Reformers had been accom-

---

1. John E. Cox, ed., *Miscellaneous Writings and Letters of Thomas Cranmer* (Cambridge: Parker Society, 1846), 345–46.

plished. Scripture was to be readily available and publicly read in the language of the common people.

Why all the fuss? Why such an ardent emphasis on access to Scripture? Why were Cambridge academics willing to suffer and die so that others could read the Bible? The answer is found in the English Reformers' understanding of the slogan *sola Scriptura*.

Five Affirmations regarding Scripture

In this chapter we will consider five affirmations regarding Scripture found in the Anglican Formularies: Scripture is God's word, Scripture is sufficient, Scripture is powerful, Scripture is satisfying, and Scripture is authoritative. These affirmations present us with a simple but profound understanding of the meaning of the phrase *sola Scriptura* in the English Reformation. Building on these affirmations, we will reflect on the significance of Scripture in the life of the Anglican Communion today and suggest how we might once again elevate the principle of *sola Scriptura* through biblical preaching, biblical scholarship, and the regular reading of Scripture by all God's people.

SCRIPTURE IS GOD'S WORD

Reader: The word of the Lord.
Congregation: Thanks be to God.

Anyone who has ever worshiped in an Anglican setting knows these words well. At the end of every Scripture reading we are reminded that what we have heard is God's own Word, and we respond by giving thanks.

To understand the passion of the Reformers one must recognize this fundamental belief that the Bible is the "word of God written." The Book of Homilies begins with a sermon entitled "A Fruitful Exhortation to the Reading of Holy Scripture" (hereafter, "Homily on Scripture"). It is no coincidence that this, the first of the published formularies, begins with an address explaining the significance of Scripture in the life of the church. Almost certainly the work of Thomas Cranmer, the opening line of the homily reads, "Unto a Christian man there can be nothing either more necessary or profitable than the knowledge of Holy Scripture: forasmuch as in it is contained God's true Word, setting forth his glory and also man's duty."[2]

Scripture is God's revelation of himself to humankind. It is his chosen means for sharing with us his being and his love. The first homily affirms that in the Old and New Testaments, "we shall find the Father, *from* whom, the Son, *by* whom, and the Holy Ghost, *in* whom all things have their being and conservation, and those three persons to be but one God and one substance." The Bible is not merely man's reflections on God, nor an attempt by human authors to describe divine reality. It is God's own self-disclosure to us. Even that most difficult doctrine of the Trinity was ultimately not the decision of a church council. The fathers merely ratified what could be plainly deduced from Scripture.

For this reason, when it came to Scripture, the initial goal of the English Reformers was not explanation but proclamation. They believed that the Bible alone was God's power for salvation, open to anyone, and that it could stand on its own. They believed that it was effective not primarily through the agency of preachers or theologians but by the power of the Holy Spirit. For God's Spirit goes forth with his words, just as human breath carries our speech to the ears of others when we speak. Since God has appointed the Scriptures as a "sure and certain" "divine instrument for salvation," the Reformers were convinced that the Bible possesses the unique power to grab hold of human hearts and turn them to the love of Christ.

Scripture does not, therefore, require the mediating agency of the church or elaborate explanation by a scholar for it to be received faithfully. It is God's direct address to all human beings. This is not

---

2. Ronald B. Bond, *Certain Sermons or Homilies (1547) and A Homily against Disobedience and Wilful Rebellion (1570): A Critical Edition* (Toronto: University of London Press, 1987), 61 (the English in all quotations from this text has been modernized).

to say that the Reformers were naïve simpletons when it came to the often difficult work of interpreting the meaning of Scripture— many were biblical scholars of the highest order! It is, rather, the affirmation that as God's word to his people, Scripture is effective in revealing God's identity, his glory, his love, and his plan for our redemption. Naturally, part of this plan is showing us how much we are not like God right now, even as he assures us that he will ultimately transform us into the image of Christ.

In affirming Scripture as the Word of God, the Reformers asserted its *uniqueness* and its *unity*. These qualities are set out in particular in the Thirty-Nine Articles. On the one hand, the *uniqueness* of Scripture is explained in Article 6:

> Holy Scripture containeth all things necessary to salvation: so that whatsoever is not read therein, nor may be proved thereby, is not to be required of any man, that it should be believed as an article of the faith, or be thought requisite or necessary to salvation. In the name of Holy Scripture, we do understand those Canonical books of the Old and New Testament, of whose authority was never any doubt in the Church.

Article 6 goes on to list the canonical books of the Old Testament, agreed upon by all Protestants, and to affirm the canon of the New Testament, universally agreed upon by the church. Because Scripture alone reveals God's saving grace in Jesus Christ, it is unique. It cannot be amended or diminished. The canon is closed.

On the other hand, the *unity* of Scripture is affirmed in Article 7: "The Old Testament is not contrary to the New; for both in the Old and New Testament everlasting life is offered to mankind by Christ, who is the only Mediator between God and man, being both God and man." This unique word of God that proclaims salvation through Jesus Christ is unified in its message. It is coherent and noncontradictory. Because of the unity of Scripture, Article 20 declares that "it is not lawful for the Church to ordain any thing that is contrary to God's Word written, *neither may it so expound one place of Scripture, that it be repugnant to another"* (emphasis added). This affirmation of Scripture's unity was in part a reaction against the Roman Catholics' use of James's call for works to undermine Paul's insistence on salvation as a free gift. Moreover, the English Reformers utterly rejected the tendencies among the more radical Reformers to discount the revelation of God in the Old Testament. The Articles unabashedly affirm the authority of the Old Testament and its ongoing relevance in the story of salvation. Scripture is a whole that must not be divided.

Richard Hooker, the late-sixteenth-century defender of the Reformation, described the unity of Scripture this way:

> The general end of both old and new is one, the difference between them consisting in this, that the old did make wise by teaching salvation through Christ should come, the new by teaching the Christ the Saviour is come, and that Jesus whom the Jews did crucify, and whom God did raise again from the dead is he.[3]

The Anglican poet and priest George Herbert gave expression to the principle of Scripture's unity in his poem *The Holy Scriptures II*:

> Oh that I knew how all thy lights combine,
>   And the configurations of their glorie!
>   Seeing not onely how each verse doth shine,
> But all the constellations of the storie.
> This verse marks that, and both do make a motion
>   Unto a third, that ten leaves off doth lie;
>   Then as dispersed herbs to watch a potion,
> These three make up some Christians destinie.

The English Reformers believed that Scripture is "God's word written," his revelation of himself to all people. It is unique and the

---

3. Richard Hooker, *Of the Laws of Ecclesiastical Polity*, in *The Folger Library Edition of the Works of Richard Hooker*, ed. Speed Hill (Cambridge, MA: Belknap, 1977), I.14.4; 1:128. The first reference uses the passage numbering system in John Keble, ed., *The Works of . . . Mr. Richard Hooker*, 7th ed., rev. R. W. Church and F. Paget (Oxford, 1888).

message it proclaims is unified, reflecting the united being of God the three-in-one.

At the heart of this affirmation is an awesome truth: God pursues us. It is God who speaks and God who seeks. Through Scripture God reaches out and draws us to himself. In faith we respond to his initiative. The Anglican approach to Scripture is characterized by awestruck wonder that God would so graciously pursue us with his love. For this reason we receive Scripture with reverence and with joy. It animates our liturgies and gives rhythm to our daily life. Indeed, in the chapter on *sola gratia,* we shall see how Thomas Cranmer used the four Bible verses of his Comfortable Words to draw the hearts of the congregation heavenward during Holy Communion. Therefore, Cranmer is right to exhort us in the homily on Scripture, "Let us thank God heartily for this his great and special gift, beneficial favor and fatherly providence. Let us be glad to revive this precious gift of our heavenly father."[4]

Scripture Is Sufficient

If any thing be necessary to be learned, of the holy Scripture we may learn it.[5]

Thus said Thomas Cranmer in his 1540 preface to the Great Bible, expressing the principle, found throughout the formularies, that Scripture is *sufficient.* To speak of the sufficiency of Scripture is both an affirmation and a qualification. It is entirely sufficient for redemption but not exhaustive concerning everything in life.

In the words of the "Homily on Scripture," "there is no truth, nor doctrine, necessary for our justification and everlasting salvation, but that is, or may be, drawn out of that fountain and well of truth." The homily continues, "For in Holy Scripture is fully contained what we ought to do and what to eschew, what to believe, what to love and what to look for at God's hands at length."[6] Scripture is

---

4. Bond, *Certain Sermons or Homilies,* 66.

5. Cox, *Miscellaneous Writings and Letters of Thomas Cranmer,* 121.

6. Ibid., 61–62.

sufficient because it communicates and explains all matters central to salvation, covering both faith and morals.

An important aspect of the sufficiency of Scripture is its clarity. The traditional term used to express this is *perspicuity* (from Latin, *perspicuus*, meaning "transparent" or "clear"). When it comes to the essential matters of salvation and the nature of the Christian life, the Bible not only contains all necessary truth; it also communicates these truths clearly and distinctly. As Cranmer wrote in his personal notes:

> All Scripture is divinely inspired, etc. . . . that whatsoever truth is necessary to be taught for our salvation, or the contrary to be reproved, whatsoever is necessary for us to do, and what to forbear and not to do, all is completely contained in the Scripture, so that a man thereby may be perfectly instructed unto all manner of goodness.[7]

The humble, patient hearer of the text is not left ignorant or ill-informed, but holds in his or her hand knowledge of the essential truth of God's self-revelation and the right course of action that must be taken in response. In his preface to the Great Bible, Cranmer quotes John Chrysostom to this effect: "The apostles and prophets wrote their books so, that their special intent and purpose might be understood and perceived of every reader; which was nothing but the edification or amendment of the life of them that read or hear it."[8] Cranmer made the same point again in the "Homily on Scripture": "There is no thing spoken under dark mysteries in one place, but the self same thing in other places is spoken more familiarly and plainly, to the capacity both of learned and unlearned."[9]

To say that Scripture is sufficient is a resounding affirmation of its content and clarity, but it is also a qualification. For the Anglican

---

7. Thomas Cranmer, "Cranmer's Great Commonplaces," British Library, Royal Manuscript 7.B.XI, 46r (the English has been modernized).

8. G. E. Duffield, ed., *The Works of Thomas Cranmer*, with introduction by J. I. Packer (Philadelphia: Fortress, 1965), 35 (the English in this text has been modernized).

9. Bond, *Certain Sermons or Homilies*, 66.

Reformers, Scripture is not comprehensive. Not all knowledge is to be found therein. Scripture is silent on certain matters, and our own wise and well-considered reflections on matters not directly addressed by Scripture are necessary. It is meant to be supplemented by human reflection, philosophy, the natural sciences, and, in matters of church life, Christian tradition.

There is no more eloquent application of this understanding of Scripture's sufficiency than in Hooker's *Laws of Ecclesiastical Polity* (1594–1597), a multivolume treatise in which he clearly sets forth the salvation-sufficiency of Scripture alongside the necessity of extra-scriptural reflection on church government and ceremonies. Here Hooker models the careful study and application of Scripture in an area of ecclesial life where various interpretations are possible. In order to do so, Hooker employs the use of reason and tradition. To tease out the implications of Scripture in a debated area, he uses "theological reason," that is, his own natural ability, steeped in and transformed by meditating on different passages of Scripture. He then seeks wisdom and input from the reflections and decisions of previous generations of Christians.

Anglicans often refer to the image of the three-legged stool, where Scripture, tradition, and reason stand as legs supporting the life of the church. This popular image is generally traced back to Hooker, who is said to be an exemplar of the model. It is, however, misleading. In this image Scripture, tradition, and reason stand as equal partners in the task of guiding and informing Christ's church; each one retains its own autonomy and authority equal to the others. Scripture is treated as one source among several of God's unique wisdom for his people. This is not an accurate picture of what Hooker is doing in his magisterial work. A better picture of the relationship between Scripture, tradition, and reason is offered by Ashley Null:

> Although it is common among Anglicans to speak of the three-legged stool of Scripture, Tradition and Reason, in which each

leg is equal, it is far more accurate to speak of Scripture as a garden bed in which reason and tradition are tools used to tend the soil, unlock its nutrients and bring forth the beauty within it.[10]

Scripture is sufficient. It contains all matters necessary for salvation and communicates clearly. On secondary matters where Scripture is silent or its meaning debated, we are right to use the tools God has given us to turn over the rich soil of his Word, comparing text with text, viewing matters through the lens of the church's tradition, and applying the careful scrutiny of reason in order to discover God's will for us.

That Scripture is sufficient is not merely a theological assertion; it is a comfort and a charge. As we said, clarity is at the heart of the sufficiency of Scripture. The message of salvation and the means by which Christ redeems are clear to anyone who reads the Gospels with an open heart and mind. Moreover, the response demanded by the offer of salvation is also clear: faith in the Son of God! While preachers may at times muddle the message of the gospel, Scripture is always clear. It does not allow itself to be read merely as a work of literature or history. It naturally brings those who read it to a place of decision and accountability. The all-sufficient Word of God confronts readers with a choice: believe or not. And when, by the gracious work of the Holy Spirit, the choice has been made to repent and believe, the fruit is a confident faith. The clarity of Scripture begets a confident faith.

Confidence, however, does not breed arrogance. For, while Scripture contains all things necessary for our salvation, it is not a complete revelation of God. Remember, to say that Scripture is sufficient implies a qualification: it is not exhaustive. Just as Scripture is limited in content, so are we limited in comprehension and experience. Inasmuch as we are fallen creatures on the way to full redemption, our knowledge of God and experience of him are par-

---

10. Ashley Null, *"Sola Scriptura"* (lecture presented at the synod of the Diocese of the Carolinas [ACNA], Mount Pleasant, South Carolina, October 29, 2015).

tial and will become complete only in the new creation. This truth ought to bring forth in us a sense of humble expectation, seen in our willingness to struggle together to address those things left unclear in Scripture, our active dependence on the Holy Spirit as our guide, and our ultimate confidence that God will reveal and assert himself in the church.

Scripture Is Powerful

> In the beginning God created the heavens and the earth. The earth was without form and void, and darkness was over the face of the deep. And the Spirit of God was hovering over the face of the waters.
>
> And God said, "Let there be light," and there was light. (Gen. 1:1–3)

Scripture begins with the mighty voice of God speaking into the void and calling creation into existence. The firm conviction of the Anglican Reformers was that this same voice, in the fullness of its power, still speaks through the written word of God in Scripture. As the author of the letter to the Hebrews says, "The word of God is living and active, sharper than any two-edged sword, piercing to the division of soul and of spirit, of joints and of marrow, and discerning the thoughts and intentions of the heart" (Heb. 4:12). What was true for the first-century church was also true for the sixteenth-century church and remains true today. In the "Homily on Scripture," Cranmer affirms this power:

> The words of Holy Scripture be called words of everlasting life: for they be God's instrument, ordained for the same purpose. They have power to convert through God's promise and they be effectual through God's assistance; and, being received in a faithful heart, they have ever an heavenly spiritual working in them.[11]

---

11. Bond, *Certain Sermons or Homilies*, 62.

The Bible is not a magical text exercising its power through mantras or magnetism. It is, rather, a spiritual text, effective through the agency of the Holy Spirit who caused it to be written and now causes it to be understood. As Cranmer says later in the same homily, the Spirit "inspires the true sense to those who with humility and diligence do search thereof."[12] In the care of the Holy Spirit, Scripture is the living and powerful word of God. That power is particularly evident in two ways: conversion and transformation.

Thomas Bilney, Cambridge scholar and humble encourager of the Reformation, described his own conversion in the following manner:

> I chanced upon this sentence of St. Paul (Oh most sweet and comfortable sentence to my soul!) in 1 Tim. 1:15: "It is a true saying and worthy of all men to be embraced, that Christ Jesus came into the world to save sinners, of whom I am the chief and principal." This one sentence, through God's instruction . . . working inwardly in my heart, did so gladden it—which before was wounded by an awareness of my sins almost to the point of desperation—that immediately I felt a marvelous inner peace, so much so that my bruised bones leapt for joy.[13]

For Bilney, Scripture was not merely a source of infallible knowledge. It was a powerful tool in the hands of the Holy Spirit that brought about his personal conversion. Because it is the divine voice speaking through the written words of men, Scripture is effective in the same way that God's voice spoken into the darkness brought forth light and earth. It can speak to hearts of stone and turn them to hearts of flesh. We must not, therefore, underestimate the power of Scripture in the work of evangelism.

In the Western world there is sometimes a negative association between evangelism and Scripture. Far too many soapbox preachers have harangued the masses with shouted declamations

---

12. Ibid., 66. Cranmer is quoting Chrysostom, *On Genesis*, Homily 21.
13. John Foxe, *Actes and Monuments* (London: John Day, 1570), 1141–43 (the text has been modernized).

of quoted Scripture in a way that feels forced and foreign in our pluralist societies. When divorced from the life and witness of the speaker, Scripture can appear as merely a tool of religious propaganda. As a result, many Christians turn to their own summaries and explanations of Scripture in private conversation in an effort to make sharing the gospel more natural and accessible. This can be fine and good, but in this work of accommodation, the powerful clarity of God's own Word is all too often lost. Scripture is not a blunt instrument used to beat down or convince. It is a life-giving word, imbued with the power of God's Spirit and available to be shared humbly, openly, and honestly. For it still possesses the power to convert even the hardest of hearts.

The Spirit's work through Scripture is not complete at conversion but continues in the transformation of those who hear and read it. In the second Book of Homilies, issued under Elizabeth I, a new sermon on Scripture was included, most likely composed by Bishop John Jewel. He writes, "Let every man, woman and child therefore with all their heart thirst and desire God's holy Scriptures, love them, embrace them, have their delight and pleasure in hearing and reading them; so as at length we may be transformed and change into them."[14]

When Scripture is read, studied, and embraced, it works in our hearts and minds to convert our affections. In this digital age, one might say that Scripture has the power, in the hands of the Spirit, to reconfigure our hardware, not just our software. The first homily on Scripture says, "This Word whosoever is diligent to read and in his heart to print that he readeth, the great affection to the transitory things of this world shall be diminished in him, and the great desire of heavenly things that be therein promised of God shall increase in him."[15] Regular exposure to Scripture works to change our most basic desires. And when our affections are converted, action soon follows: "For that thing which by perpetual use of reading of Holy

---

14. John Griffiths, ed., *The Two Books of Homilies Appointed to Be Read in Churches* (Oxford: Oxford University Press, 1859), 370.

15. Bond, *Certain Sermons or Homilies*, 63.

Scripture and diligent searching of the same is deeply printed and graven in the heart at length turns almost into nature."[16] Scripture has the power, through the work of the Spirit, to reshape our affections and transform our actions.

Thomas Cranmer had this principle in mind when he composed the Book of Common Prayer. In one of the collects to be prayed regularly at the discretion of the minister, Cranmer wrote, "Grant, we beseech thee, Almighty God, that the words which we have heard this day, with our outward ears, may through thy grace be so grafted inwardly in our hearts, that they may bring forth in us the fruit of good living."[17] One of Cranmer's goals in writing and revising the Book of Common Prayer was to get Scripture into the ears of the people so that their hearts might be turned to God and their lives transformed by his love. Cranmer argues that this desire was also the intent of the early Fathers of the church in laying out ordered prayers and readings:

> For they so ordered the matter, that all the whole Bible (or the greatest part thereof) should be read over once in the year intending thereby, that the clergy, and especially such as were ministers of the congregation, should (by often reading and meditation of God's word) be stirred up to godliness themselves, and be more able also to exhort other by wholesome doctrine, and to confute them that were adversaries to the truth. And further, that the people (by daily hearing of holy Scripture read in the Church) should continually profit more and more in the knowledge of God, and be the more inflamed with the love of his true religion.[18]

Far too often we treat Scripture merely as a source of knowledge that guides doctrine and is useful in shaping our view of the world.

---

16. Ibid.

17. Joseph Ketley, ed., *The Two Liturgies . . . in the Reign of King Edward the Sixth* (Cambridge: Parker Society, 1844), 281–82.

18. Cranmer's preface to the Book of Common Prayer (1552), in ibid., 13 (the English in the text has been modernized.)

But Scripture is much more than this. It works not just in our minds to shape our thoughts but also on our hearts to shape our desires. This is why we memorize it. This is why we set its verses to song and sing them out loud. This is why we study it and meditate on it. We come to Scripture with humble hearts and pray that by the power of the Holy Spirit the words planted within us would work to transform us into the glory of the risen Christ.

Scripture is powerful for personal transformation. But it does not stop there. The Reformers believed that Scripture was powerful to effect widespread social transformation as well. A generation after Cranmer, John Jewel gave eloquent voice to this hope in his *Treatise on Holy Scripture* (1570):

> But when the fullness of time came, God sent forth his word, and all was changed. Error fell down, and truth stood up: men forsook their idols, and went to God. The kings, and priests, and people were changed: the temples, and sacrifices, and prayers were changed: men's eyes and hearts were changed. They forsook their gods, their kings, their priests: they forsook their antiquity, customs, consent, their fathers, and themselves. What power was able to work these things? What emperor by force ever prevailed so much? What strength could ever shake down so mighty idols from their seat? What hand of man could subdue and conquer the whole world, and make such mighty nations confess they had done amiss? This did the Lord bring to pass by the power of his word, and the breath of his mouth.[19]

There is not space here to elaborate on the Reformers' expectation that a converted people would produce a more righteous nation. Let it suffice to say that their belief in the power of Scripture was not limited to simple personal conversion, nor merely to individual change, but envisioned widespread social transformation among God's people.

---

19. John Jewel, *The Works of John Jewel, D.D., Bishop of Salisbury*, ed. Richard William Jelf, 8 vols. (Oxford: Oxford University Press, 1848), 7:292–93.

In recent decades no other Anglican has demonstrated the power of this conviction as forcefully as John Stott in his book *Issues Facing Christians Today*. The longtime rector of All Souls, Langham Place, London, Stott first published this tome in the early 1980s. Over the next two decades the book underwent two revisions at his hand. It is a monumental work of biblical exegesis and social commentary. In it, Stott addresses complex and challenging social issues ranging from sexuality to nuclear disarmament to care for the environment. Each issue receives careful analysis followed by clear biblical teaching, thoughtful reflection, and, finally, carefully considered suggestions for action and application. Operating under the principle that Scripture has the power to transform nations, Stott models the journey from exegesis to application with unparalleled sensitivity and wisdom. In doing so, he calls the church to action and holds the nation-state to account. This is the power of Scripture.

Scripture Is Satisfying

In the Scriptures are the fat pastures of the soul.[20]

God's word in Scripture is sufficient and powerful. It is also deeply satisfying, like a multicourse meal. Throughout the Anglican Formularies, Scripture is metaphorically described as food and drink, a refrain that emphasizes the delight with which we are nourished by God's Word. In his preface to the Homilies in 1547, Edward VI describes Scripture as "the very Word of God, that lively food of man's soul." The "Homily on Scripture" claims that, "as drink is pleasant to them that be dry, and meat to them that be hungry, so is the reading, hearing, searching, and studying of Holy Scripture to them that be desirous to know God or themselves, and to do his will."[21] The "Homily on Good Works," refers to the "sweet and savory bread of God's own word."[22]

---

20. Thomas Cranmer, "Preface to the Great Bible," in Duffield, *The Works of Thomas Cranmer*, 37 (the English in this text has been modernized).

21. Bond, *Certain Sermons or Homilies*, 55, 61.

22. Ibid., 112.

Food metaphors abound in the writings of the Anglican Reformers, revealing a profound understanding of the nature of Scripture. It is, in a very basic sense, essential to our survival. We cannot live and thrive as human beings created in the image of God without it. Cranmer understood this well. The daily rhythm of worship contained in the Book of Common Prayer serves up regular meals of Scripture through the language of the liturgy, which abounds with phrases and imagery taken directly from God's Word. Continuing the tradition of the church from ancient times, Cranmer also compiled a lectionary for daily worship in which Scripture is poured into the hearts and minds of God's people as daily bread. Each month the entire Psalter is consumed. The Old and New Testaments are devoured in their entirety throughout the course of each year. Day in and day out a steady diet of God's life-giving Word is fed to his people. The sheer quantity of Scripture read in the weekly cycle of worship ensures that we eat our fill. It is to be read in volume, consumed amid the rigors of daily life, and used for energy and nourishment across all spheres, both secular and sacred.

There is, however, a warning we must heed along with this basic conviction about the nature of Scripture. Without the sustenance that it provides we grow hungry and become spiritually famished, desperate for nourishment of any kind. In the absence of Scripture, we feed our souls with the equivalent of spiritual junk food. We turn to "self-help," the prosperity gospel, social movements that promise liberation, and other excesses of the unchecked will. As we feed on these fraudulent replacements of God's Word, our spiritual health declines into ruin. Only God's Word can satisfy our daily needs.

While the daily reading of Scripture is a discipline to be encouraged for the health of all people, it is not merely this. It is also a feast to be enjoyed. This is easily forgotten by the earnest Christian who reads Scripture as if he were taking his daily vitamins. To say that Scripture is satisfying signifies not only that it is a necessary part of our spiritual diet, but also that it is a lip-smacking feast of nourishment, "the sweet and savory bread of God's own word." Scripture is necessary sustenance for the human soul that is not only healthy but tasty as well!

SCRIPTURE IS AUTHORITATIVE

> The Church hath power to decree rites or ceremonies and authority in controversies of faith; and yet it is not lawful for the Church to ordain anything contrary to God's word written, neither may it so expound one place of Scripture, that it be repugnant to another. Wherefore, although the Church be a witness and a keeper of Holy Writ: yet, as it ought not to decree anything against the same, so besides the same ought it not to enforce anything to be believed for necessity of salvation. (Article 20 of the Thirty-Nine Articles)

At the heart of the Reformation debates was the question of authority. The Anglican Reformers understood that it was essential to their task to reaffirm Scripture's authority over the church, thus reversing centuries of practice in which the institutional church held pride of place when it came to final authority. Cranmer, writing in his personal notebooks (the "Great Commonplaces"), says, "Scripture comes not from the church, but from God and has authority by the Holy Spirit."[23] Elsewhere he expands on the theme: "Authority of the Scriptures is from God, the author, and not from man.... The authority of Scripture ought not to be made subordinate to the judgments of the church, but the church itself ought to be judged and governed by the Scriptures."[24]

We see the application of this conviction throughout the Anglican Formularies, in both their shape and content. That the very first of the Homilies is the "Homily on Scripture" is no accident. Homilies 4, 9, and 10 refer to Scripture as "infallible," a term regularly applied to Scripture in the works of the Reformers. J. I. Packer, in his exposition of the Thirty-Nine Articles, comments, "The authority of ecclesiasti-

---

23. Cranmer, "Cranmer's Great Commonplaces," trans. Ashley Null from the original Latin, 8v.
24. Ibid., 32v.

cal statements of faith is . . . the derived authority of a faithful echo, exposition, and application of 'God's Word written' in its witness to God's living and personal Word, His own Son."[25] He goes on to say, "The Creeds and the Articles alike come to us as venerable commentaries on, and primary expositions of, Holy Scripture; no more, and no less."[26] This is made abundantly clear in the Royal Declaration of 1628, still affixed to the Articles in 1662, which states, "The Articles of the Church of England . . . do contain the true Doctrine of the Church of England agreeable to God's Word: which we do therefore ratify and confirm." Scripture is rule and guide for the Articles.

If Scripture is authoritative for the church, then all other authority in the church depends on faithfulness to the living word of Scripture. Oliver O'Donovan, in his reflections on the Articles, helpfully clarifies the relationship between Scripture and church: "Scripture is independent of, and prior to, the church's exposition of Scripture . . . the implication is clear: the books of Scripture are not authoritative because the Church views them in a certain way; the Church views them in a certain way because they are authoritative."[27]

If this is true, then the hallmark of godly human authority is humble submission to God's Word. This is nowhere more evident than in Cranmer's Ordinal, first published in 1550 and subsequently revised. In his appropriation of the medieval rites for ordination, Cranmer does a masterful job of paring back and simplifying. He also defines the ministry of the ordained in the context of a priest's relationship to Scripture. In the 1552 revision of the Ordinal, Cranmer omits the giving of chalice and paten to the newly ordained, leaving only the gift of the Bible. Scripture is the primary authority under which a priest serves and the principal gift a priest is to share.

In the initial charge to the ordinand in the 1662 Book of Common Prayer, the bishop says:

25. J. I. Packer, "The Status of the Articles," in H. E. W. Turner et al., *The Articles of the Church of England* (London: Mowbray, 1964), 45.

26. Ibid., 47.

27. Oliver O'Donovan, *On the Thirty-Nine Articles: A Conversation with Tudor Christianity*, 2nd ed. (London: SCM, 2011), 46.

And seeing that you cannot by any other means compass the doing of so weighty a work, pertaining to the salvation of man, but with doctrine and exhortation taken out of the Holy Scriptures, and with a life agreeable to the same; consider how studious you should be in reading and learning the Scriptures, and in framing the manners both of yourselves, and of those that especially pertain to you, according to the rule of the same Scriptures; and for this self-same cause, how you should forsake and set aside, as much as you may, all worldly cares and studies.[28]

During the ordination examination the candidate is asked:

Are you persuaded that the Holy Scriptures contain all Doctrine required as necessary for eternal salvation through faith in Jesus Christ? And are you determined, out of the said Scriptures to instruct the people committed to your charge; and to teach nothing, as necessary to eternal salvation, but that which you shall be persuaded may be concluded and proved by the Scripture?

Candidates respond, "I am so persuaded, and have so determined, by God's grace."

The ministry of a priest, like the ministry of the church itself, is the humble and grateful dispensing of Scripture. This is no mere book of rules, but as I have argued above, it is the living word of God, sufficient for salvation, powerful for conversion and transformation, satisfying to the spiritually hungry, and authoritative for doctrine and practice.

Sola Scriptura in Practice

When the Great Bible was published in 1539, it was produced with an elaborate woodcut illustration on the title page. At the very top of the page God himself is pictured, arms spread wide in the act of bestowing his word. A kneeling King Henry VIII receives the divine word, repeating the words of Psalm 119:105 as he does, "Your word

---

28. The English in this text has been modernized.

is a lamp to my feet . . ." Immediately below this scene the king sits astride his throne in the top center of the page, handing copies of Scripture to Cromwell on his left and Cranmer on his right. In these two men all people, both laity and clergy, are represented. Moving down the page, Cranmer is shown delivering the Bible to a priest, who in the next scene down is pictured preaching to the masses. On the right side, Cromwell is shown delivering the Bible to the representatives of the people, who in the scene below cry out in gratitude, "God save the king!"

The woodcut is a marvelous example of the artist's skill and a surprisingly useful tool for assessing the practical implications of the distribution of Scripture in the plain language of the people. Having seen what the Reformation cry *sola Scriptura* meant for the Reformers of the church in England, we now turn to consider how this understanding shapes our approach to Anglican life and worship today. Three areas call for comment: preaching, study, and scholarship, each of which is symbolized in the famous woodcut on the title page of the Great Bible.

BIBLICAL PREACHING

Scripture must be publicly proclaimed. This is the undeniable point of the progression of images on the title page of the Great Bible. When Cranmer hands the Bible to a priest, the priest knows exactly what to do. From a raised pulpit he preaches, and those gathered below receive the Word with gratitude.

From our earliest days, Anglicans have been a people who emphasize biblical preaching and teaching. The very first of the Anglican Formularies to be published and circulated by Archbishop Cranmer after the coronation of Edward VI was the Book of Homilies. This collection of sermons was to be delivered in every parish church in the country and contained the essence of the Reformed doctrine of the church. Weekly preaching of God's Word was seen as *the* primary method of communication and instruction in the Edwardian church.

In his preface to the Homilies, Edward VI describes their purpose as "the true setting forth and pure declaring of God's Word, which is the principal guide and leader unto all godliness and virtue." In this phrase he sets forth an agenda for biblical preaching. He affirms the priority and authority of Scripture, along with its effect on the hearts, minds, and actions of men, and characterizes preaching as the clear setting forth of its meaning. What is preaching? Quite simply, "the true setting forth and pure declaring of God's Word."[29]

Luminaries such as Hugh Latimer, Charles Simeon, and John Stott were among the most well-known Anglicans of their day, known principally for their faithful, eloquent, and practical expositions of Scripture. If the Anglican Communion is to have a healthy and vibrant future, it must reassert the centrality of biblical preaching in the life of the church. This comes at a cost. The preparation and delivery of clear, biblical sermons requires time, training, and resources. In the training of clergy and lay leaders, preaching must be given prominence. Theological education must consist of adequate instruction in biblical languages where at all possible, access to high-quality resources of biblical scholarship and scriptural commentary, and the modeling of excellent preaching in the cultural context in which leaders are being trained to serve. Those called to ministry as leaders in local churches must give priority to sermon preparation and personal study of Scripture. If preaching is at the heart of Reformation Anglicanism, then time in the study must be at the center of an Anglican pastor's life!

Strong encouragement to faithful preaching is given to us by Hugh Latimer and Charles Simeon. In a sermon before Edward VI on April 5, 1549, Latimer said, "I told you before of the ladder of heaven; I would you should not forget it. The steps thereof are set forth in the tenth [chapter] to the Romans. The first is preaching, then hearing, then believing and last of all salvation. . . . God's in-

---

29. Bond, *Certain Sermons or Homilies*, 55.

strument of salvation is preaching."[30] Simeon, in reflecting on the liturgy of the church, said:

> Here let us pause a moment, to reflect, what stress our Reformers laid on the Holy Scriptures, as the only sure directory for our faith and practice, and the only certain rule of all our ministrations. They have clearly given it as their sentiment, that to study the word of God ourselves, and to open it to others, is the proper labour of a minister; a labour, that calls for all his time, and all his attention.[31]

Scripture is the bedrock of all faithful preaching, but for many people the Word of God is foreign and distant. Only through patient and clear exegesis is it brought into the lives of those who sit in cathedral pews or on the hard-packed dirt floor of a village church. Careful exposition of a biblical book or epistle week by week opens up the world of Scripture and invites people to participate in it themselves. When entire books of the Bible are sequentially laid open before a people gathered in worship, that community is formed in the rhythm of God's sufficient Word. This kind of expository preaching is good food for God's people. But preaching cannot merely be expository. It must also be gospel-shaped and gospel-driven. The task of the preacher is not solely to open Scripture and explain and teach it, but also to draw out the threads of the gospel story week in and week out as it finds its culmination in Christ.

The Homilies are not a model of this kind of text-centered, expository preaching. They are, instead, a model of systematic gospel proclamation. The Homilies make clear that the good news of Jesus Christ is his atoning sacrifice for a humanity held captive by the guilt and power of sin so that they might be restored to fellowship with God, one another, and their true selves by trusting in Christ's

---

30. In Arthur Pollard, ed., *Hugh Latimer: The Sermons* (Manchester: Carcanet/Fyfield, 2002), 58.

31. Charles Simeon, *The Excellence of the Liturgy* (1812), quoted in Andrew Atherstone, *Charles Simeon on "The Excellence of the Liturgy,"* Joint Liturgical Studies 72 (Norwich: Hymns Ancient and Modern, 2011), 48.

promise of free forgiveness and newness of life. As such they are a helpful reminder of the place and purpose of preaching in the life of a people. Preaching takes place in the context of worship and must lead a congregation to worship. In order to accomplish this, it cannot merely be practical or informative; it must proclaim the gospel. Cranmer understood this, and in laying out the Homilies, he placed into the hands of every pastor-preacher a model for doing so. The Homilies themselves need not be the vehicle by which one does this. Their sixteenth-century English and complex sentence structure do not communicate particularly well in most contexts today. What they do accomplish, however, is profound. They remind all preachers that their task is to proclaim the life-saving, world-changing work of God in Christ accomplished through his life, death, and resurrection. This is the food that feeds and nourishes God's people when they gather to worship. Faithful preaching is gospel proclamation and is thus the primary task for leaders in Christ's church.

BIBLICAL STUDY

Perhaps the most shocking aspect of the title page of the Great Bible was that the people—not just the clergy—were given God's Word and invited to "read, mark, learn and inwardly digest," as Cranmer put it so well in his Collect for the Second Sunday in Advent. In a later work, Foxe's *Acts and Monuments*, a similarly evocative illustration adorns the title page. Once again a preacher stands in a pulpit proclaiming God's Word to the people. In this illustration a number of those listening hold copies of Scripture in their hands. One prominently portrayed woman is shown reading along in her Bible as she listens. The images are instructive. Scripture is meant to be consumed not just through the refined preaching of pastors and teachers but by all believers. This happens in private devotion, small group study, and corporate worship. We look at each briefly.

In the Book of Common Prayer, Cranmer retained the structure of daily morning and evening worship crafted by the early and medieval church. Clergy were required to say Morning and Evening Prayer and, whenever possible, to do so in the parish church, where others could join them. Daily prayer was not merely for the clergy; it was for everyone. This set rhythm of daily life is rarely observed in Anglican circles today. The busyness of modern life militates against set-aside times of prayer and reading. The church is weaker for this loss. And while we need not necessarily bring back the practice of Morning and Evening Prayer, we must encourage the daily reading and studying of Scripture by all people. The cultivation of a devotional life is essential to the health and well-being of individual Christians and to the church as a whole. If the Bible is indeed God's living word, it must be consumed! Implicit within this emphasis on devotional Bible reading is a necessary concern for literacy and translation. Anglican churches and missions serve the good of local communities by working for universal literacy and by engaging in the slow and painstaking work of rendering Scripture in the local language.

One of the great gifts of the modern evangelical movement is the advent of the small group Bible study. While private devotion encourages daily nourishment and regular intercession, a deeper engagement with Scripture is possible in the context of small group studies, where individuals come together to discuss, search, and apply God's Word. Studies like this are important because they do not depend on clerical leadership. Instead, they affirm the right and duty of all Christian people to wrestle with Scripture. Furthermore, they remind us that Scripture is given to the community and not just to individuals. Particularly in Western cultures, which emphasize the autonomy of the individual, Christians easily become isolated interpreters of the text, prone to the kind of heresies Cranmer's opponents were rightly wary of. In this context, group discussion, debate, and investigation are crucial to a shared humility before God and one another. If Scripture is central to our Anglican identity, it must be consumed around a common table.

Finally, one of the most significant places we feast on God's

Word is in weekly corporate worship. This happens in the preaching, but also through the liturgy. One of the reasons our worship is liturgical is that we are biblical. Liturgy is a mechanism for Scripture reading, reflecting, singing, and memorizing. This becomes obvious when one acknowledges the sheer volume of Scripture incorporated into the set texts of our liturgies. As a small example, take Cranmer's collects written for the church year and special occasions. In these new collects added to those of the old Roman rite, one scholar notes thirty different biblical quotations in addition to allusions and references. As he says, "No one would deny that the Roman collects were ultimately biblical in inspiration. Still, they rarely echoed Holy Scripture verbatim. Freed from the restraints of an original text, the author of the new collects turned to the Bible not only for matter but also for forms of expression."[32]

In keeping with Cranmer's own insistence that the "traditions of men" may change and adapt over time and according to culture, I would not insist on the universal use of the 1662 Book of Common Prayer. However, for those involved in liturgical revision and renewal, a word of warning and encouragement is required: when revising the liturgy, take care to be as intentional as Cranmer was in filling it with Scripture! Indeed, in Cranmer's thinking, the Bible was not merely an aid to crafting liturgy, as if a beautiful form of worship was his ultimate end and biblical language was merely helpful in pursuing that purpose. Rather the reverse was true. Cranmer's goal was to unite people to God through his Word. Consequently, Cranmer wanted to write Scripture indelibly on the hearts and minds of the English people, and he decided that a comprehensive Bible-based liturgy was the best means to do so. Thus, good Anglican liturgy speaks the voice of Scripture, giving people, in their own language, a way of thinking and praying that places God's Word on their tongues and in their hearts.

---

32. James A. Devereux, "Reformed Doctrine in the Collects of the First 'Book of Common Prayer,'" *Harvard Theological Review* 58, no. 1 (1965): 49–68.

BIBLICAL SCHOLARSHIP

One final area of vital engagement is that of biblical scholarship. In the early 1960s, John Stott articulated a vision for the renewal of the church in the majority world. For the saving gospel of Jesus Christ to be faithfully preached, pastors and lay leaders must be taught the truth of the gospel. For pastors and lay leaders to be well taught, theological colleges must be well staffed by faculty committed to the primacy of Scripture. For colleges to be well staffed, faculty must be well trained. For faculty to be well trained, they must attend the very best institutions in the world, where, in the context of a caring community, they can receive instruction before returning home to teach. Out of this vision was born the Langham Scholars Program. Five decades later, more than 150 scholars have been educated at the highest levels and returned home to teach. Through the vision and generosity of this one Anglican, the quality of theological education through much of the world has radically improved.

This vision for high-level biblical scholarship must not be lost in our Anglican Communion. Ardent belief in *sola Scriptura* does not lead to a naïve fundamentalism in regard to the text of Scripture. While clear and sufficient on matters of essential importance, the Bible remains an ancient text with a complex history of transmission demanding careful interpretation. This requires theologians and biblical scholars of the highest caliber. Recruiting, training, and placing these scholars ought to remain one of our highest priorities.

One of the great strengths of the Anglican Communion when it comes to scholarly engagement with Scripture is the unity with which we speak about the authority of Scripture amid the diversity of cultural contexts where we seek to teach and apply it. If we continue to read Scripture globally in a posture of humility before the text and one another, we will guard against cultural hegemonies in biblical hermeneutics. In doing so we will give a priceless gift to the worldwide body of Christ.

The Story Yet to Be Written

We live in a world awash with ink. Scripture has never been more abundantly available. And yet the availability of Scripture does not necessarily mean that the principle of *sola Scriptura* is practiced. We have access to Scripture but often lack insight and the willingness to apply it. The hard work ahead of us is the careful study of and humble submission to God's living Word.

In the collect written for the second Sunday of Advent, Cranmer captured the Reformers' view of Scripture and established its place in Anglican worship:

> Blessed Lord, who has caused all holy Scriptures to be written for our learning: grant that we may in such wise hear, read, mark, learn, and inwardly digest them, that by patience and comfort of your holy word, we may embrace and ever hold fast the blessed hope of everlasting life, which you have given us in our Saviour Jesus Christ.[33]

Scripture contains the message of salvation for all people. It must, therefore, be read, heard, understood, and digested. The preservation and faithful proclamation of Scripture are at the heart of the church's vocation in the world. Here is the bedrock for a renewed emphasis on Reformation Anglicanism in the twenty-first century.

---

33. Ketley, *Liturgies of Edward the Sixth*, 239 (the English in this text has been modernized).

CHAPTER 4

Sola Gratia

Ashley Null

But if any man hath fallen . . . let him nevertheless hear the Word of God, so fatherly alluring us to amendment.[1]

Keeping Head and Heart Together

Of course, the English Reformers were a people of the Book.[2] They insisted that authentic Christianity gave priority to the plain sense of Scripture over everything else. The authority of Scripture was more important than traditional beliefs like purgatory, pardons, and penance. The authority of Scripture was equally more important than deeply cherished devotional practices like praying to saints and burning lights before their images. After the sword of scriptural authority

---

1. Herman von Wied, *A Simple and Religious Consultation* (London: John Day, 1547), 230v. The spelling, punctuation, and diction of all early modern sources have been modernized in this chapter.

2. This chapter is adapted from "Comfortable Words: Thomas Cranmer's Gospel Falconry," copyright J. Ashley Null, published in *Comfortable Words: Essays in Honor of Paul F. M. Zahl*, ed. John D. Koch Jr. and Todd H. W. Brewer (Eugene, OR: Pickwick, 2013).

had cut away centuries of error, the Reformers believed that only the simple message of salvation by faith in Christ alone remained.

Yet, the fact that the English Reformers were people of the Book does not mean they had no heart. Without exception, they were followers of Erasmus. This Dutch scholar rejected medieval theology precisely because its emphasis on debating intricate technicalities made no impact on the actual lives of ordinary people. Instead of useless argument, Erasmus emphasized that ministers should persuade people through the power of God's Word. Since Scripture contained the "living image of Christ's most holy mind," its message could move human feelings deeply. When people heard everything God had done for them, their hearts would be inflamed with a transforming love for God, which would encourage their human wills to choose a life of practical good works. Of course, as more people actually acted out their Christian faith, society as a whole got better, too. It was just this kind of heart-felt response to Scripture that led to the conversion of the first English Protestants.

Consider the case of Katherine Parr, the widow of Henry VIII. She used passionate language to describe her transforming encounter with Scripture:

> "Come to me all you that labor and are burdened, and I shall refresh you." What gentle, merciful, and comfortable words are these to all sinners? . . . What a most gracious comfortable, and gentle saying was this, with such pleasant and sweet words to allure his enemies to come to him? . . . When I behold the beneficence, liberality, mercy and goodness of the Lord, I am encouraged, emboldened and stirred to ask for such a noble gift as living faith. . . . By this faith I am assured: and by this assurance I feel the remission of my sins. This is it that maketh me bold. This is it that comforteth me. This is it that quencheth all despair. . . . Thus, I feel myself to come, as it were, in a new garment before God, and now by his mercy, to be taken as just and righteous.[3]

---

3. Katherine Parr, *The Lamentation of a Sinner* (London: Whitchurch, 1548), B3v, B4v–B5r, B6r.

"Pleasant and sweet words"; "I am assured"; "I feel the remission of my sins"; "I feel myself . . . in a new garment": plainly, Katherine kept head and heart together.

"Allure"

This oneness of thought and feeling can be seen in the Reformers' favorite verb to use with the gospel: *allure*. According to the Oxford English Dictionary, the word comes from the practice in falconry of casting a meat-laden lure to recall a bird of prey. Such hawking was a pursuit for gentlemen and, thus, a common recreation among the people at the court of Henry VIII. Even Thomas Cranmer, the archbishop of Canterbury, was a frequent falconer. He was well known to find refreshment after long study through hawking, for his father had made sure that his son was practiced in the sport from youth as a sign of his good birth, despite their relatively modest means.[4]

The popularity of falconry meant that *allure* was often used in early modern writing as a synonym for temptation, to draw someone into sin by baiting a person's sinful desires. Consequently, the King's Book, Henry VIII's book of Christian doctrine, translates James 1:14 as "but every man is tempted, drawn, and allured by his own concupiscence." However, *allure* could also be used to mean appealing to the senses to attract others to something positive. In a 1539 Palm Sunday sermon before Henry VIII, a bishop compared personal humility to a sweet smell hidden in a corner whose aroma allured men to seek out its source. This was an apt comparison no doubt, since it was certainly as rare at court to encounter a sweet-smelling chamber as a humble courtier.[5]

Since Erasmus emphasized persuasion over debate, he often used *allure* in this positive sense of drawing people toward embracing virtue. In the *Enchiridion*, his landmark Renaissance humanist

---

4. John Gough Nichols, ed., *Narratives of the Days of the Reformation*, first series, 77 (London: Camden Society, 1859), 239.

5. Cuthbert Tunstall, *A Sermon Made upon Palm Sunday Last Past* (London: Berthelet, 1539), B3v.

handbook for practical piety, he wrote that the purpose of true learning was "to allure very many to a Christian man's life."[6] Since Erasmus treated the word as a synonym for persuasion, his use of *allure* carried the connotation of moving people "with courtesy, gentleness and pleasures." Therefore, nothing more succinctly summarized Jesus's mission: "The son of man came forth minding to stir up this nation to the love of the heavenly doctrine . . . that he might allure them the more with his gentleness."[7]

Because justification by faith also emphasized personal faith, persuasion was just as important to Luther, if not more so. Therefore, unsurprisingly Luther also found *allure* a useful word to describe how Christ wooed sinners back to himself:

> Thus, when the shepherd finds the lost sheep again, he has no intention of pushing it away in anger once more or throwing it to a hungry wolf. Rather, all his care and concern is directed to alluring it with every possible kindness. Treating it with the upmost tenderness, he takes the lamb upon his own back, lifting it up and carrying it, until he brings the animal all the way home again.[8]

For Luther, such gentle handling was the key to people coming to personal faith: "How very kindly and lovingly does the Lord allure all hearts to himself, and in this way he stirs them to believe in him."[9]

With an endorsement by both Erasmus and Luther, it was only natural that early English evangelicals would also consider *allure* an especially apt term for expressing their understanding of the process of salvation. First, they were well aware that personal belief was naturally a product of individual conviction, not compulsion. So conversion to the truth had to come from persuasive preaching,

---

6. Erasmus, *The Manual of the Christian Knight* (London: Wynkyn de Worde, 1533), [A5]r.

7. Erasmus, *The First Volume of the Paraphrase of Erasmus upon the New Testament* (London: Whitchurch, 1548), 38r, 68v.

8. Martin Luther, *D. Martin Luthers Werke: Kritische Gesamtausgabe*, ed. J. K. F. Knaake et al., 127 vols. (Weimar: Böhlaus, 1883–2009), 36:290–91.

9. Ibid., 8:359.

not just by proclamation and punishment. Richard Taverner used *allure* to stress this point in his 1540 handbook of Sunday sermons:

> The Romish bishop errs and accomplishes nothing in that he goes about by violence to draw men to the Christian faith. For besides the preaching of the Gospel, Christ gave nothing in commission to his disciples. So they preached it accordingly to their commission and left it in men's free liberty to come to it or not. They said not, either believe it or I will kill you. So you see that infidels as Turks, Saracens, and Jews ought not violently to be drawn to our faith, but lovingly rather invited and allured.[10]

And in his book against the bishop of London, John Bale came to the same point, but rather more quickly: "The office of a Christian bishop were rather to preach than to punish, rather to feed than to famish, rather gently to allure than currishly to rebuke before the world, were he after the order of Christ and his apostles."[11]

Second, *allure* can mean persuasion by expressing gentleness and kindness toward the hearer. That, of course, fit precisely with the Protestants' understanding of salvation by grace. Earlier in the same passage, Bale explicitly linked gentleness on God's part with unmerited forgiveness: "The gentle spouse of Christ (which is his church without spot) is evermore ready to forgive, though the offence be done seventy-seven times."[12] In his book of sermons for holy days, Taverner went on to define forgiveness specifically as what God used to draw people to himself: "God freely pardoning all our sins doth allure us all, by whom he has been offended, to peace and amity."[13]

For Katherine, it was this unexpected offer of immediate unmerited reconciliation with God that first captured her attention. Until that moment when she encountered this good news, Katherine was

---

10. Richard Taverner, *The Epistles and Gospels with a Brief Postil upon the Same from after Easter till Advent* (London: Richard Bankes, 1540), 42v.

11. John Bale, *A Disclosing or Opening of the Man of Sin* (Antwerp, 1543), 31v.

12. Ibid., 31r.

13. Richard Taverner, *On Saint Andrew's Day the Gospels with Brief Sermons upon Them for All the Holy Days in the Year* (London: Richard Bankes, 1542), 49v.

not searching for God. She was confident in her own penitential works. Yet, when she read Matthew 11:28, she realized that God used "such pleasant and sweet words to allure his enemies to come to him." As we have already seen, this gentle handling of sinners by God was the origin of Thomas Cranmer's notorious lenience toward those who had wronged him personally. William Shakespeare had Henry VIII put it this way:

> Do my Lord of Canterbury
> a shrewd turn, and he is your friend for ever.[14]

For Cranmer, the inherent drawing power of divine free forgiveness was the root of all evangelism.

Third, the sense of *allure* included an appeal to the hearers' own inner longings to "feel their faith." According to Cranmer, divine gracious love inspired grateful human love. Here is the heart of the Protestant message. Love by its very nature seeks union. Implicit within the offering of the gift of love is a calling, a wooing, an alluring of the recipient's love to return to the giver of love. If God loved humanity so much as to endure the cross so that people might have assurance of everlasting life with him, to use Cranmer's words again, only those with "hearts harder than stones" would not be moved to love God in return.[15] Katherine was quite clear that such was her own experience.

> Then began I to dwell in God by charity, knowing by the loving charity of God in the remission of my sins that God is charity as St. John says. So that of my faith (whereby I came to know God and whereby it pleased God even because I trusted in him to justify me) sprang this excellent charity in my heart.[16]

Thus, for the English Reformers, to encounter unconditional divine love was to discover something deep within being touched—

---

14. William Shakespeare, *Henry VIII*, act 5, scene 3, lines 176–77.
15. John E. Cox, ed., *Miscellaneous Writings and Letters of Thomas Cranmer* (Cambridge: Parker Society, 1846), 134.
16. Katherine Parr, *The Lamentation of a Sinner*, B7v–B8r.

an unquenchable, often unexpected longing for a relationship with one's Maker being stirred up; a transforming grateful human love for God being gently drawn out; a fervent drive to express this love in all outward actions rising up and directing the remainder of their lives. Fear of punishment could not produce such an inward, all-encompassing transformation in a sinner. Only the assurance of divine love made known in free pardon had that power. Perhaps no one expressed the results of feeling the alluring nature of the gospel better than Thomas Becon, Cranmer's chaplain.

> As I may sincerely report to you the affect of my heart. Truly since you declared to us the goodness of God the Father toward us through Jesus Christ, I have felt in my heart such an earnest faith and burning love toward God and his Word, that I think a thousand fires could not pluck me away from loving him. I begin now utterly to condemn, despise, reject, cast away, and consider worthless all the pleasures of this world, [in] which I have so greatly rejoiced in times past. All the threats of God, all the displeasures of God, all the fires and pains of hell could never before this day so allure me to the love of God, as you have now done by expressing unto me the exceeding mercy and unspeakable kindness of God toward us wretched sinners, insomuch that now from my very heart I desire to know what I may do, that by some means I may show again my heart to be fully fired to seek his glory. For I now desire nothing more than the advancement of his name.[17]

"Comfortable Words"

This good news of salvation by transforming grace alone was what Cranmer summed up in the prayer book's Comfortable Words, which follow the confession and assurance of forgiveness in the Communion service. Here is the gospel according to Reformation Anglicanism.

---

17. Thomas Becon, *A Christmas Banquet Garnished with Many Pleasant and Dainty Dishes* (n.p.: John Mayler for John Gough, 1542), F4v–5r.

"Hear what comfortable words our Savior Christ says to all that truly turn to him."[18] Cranmer's opening sentence highlighted the interconnectedness of gospel, comfort, and Christ. It was, after all, an important point in dispute between the Reformers and their opponents.

Walk into any medieval parish church, and above the chancel arch was a painting of Jesus as Judge. It dominated the whole interior of the nave. There on high before every parishioner's eyes Christ sat in judgment at the general resurrection, sending some people to the devils in hell, while sending others to be welcomed by angelic choirs into heaven. Here was the high point of a "moralistic strain" in late-medieval piety, which Eamon Duffy himself admitted "could be oppressive":

> Churches contained not only the chancel-arch representation
> of the Day of Doom, with its threat of terrifying reckoning down
> to the last farthing, but wall-paintings and windows illustrating
> the deadly sins, the works of mercy, the Commandments, Christ
> wounded by sabbath-breaking, the figures of the three living
> and the three dead, or the related *danse macabre*.[19]

Indeed, the medieval church had come to rely so routinely on the terror of coming torments in the afterlife to encourage moral obedience in this life that even the very nature of purgatory changed over the centuries to reinforce it. Originally, the possibility of spiritual purification after death arose as a divine concession to mercy, offering the hope of salvation even to notorious sinners who repented only at the last minute as they lay dying. According to the doctrine of purgatory, those who waited to the point of death to make things right with God could still make satisfaction for their sins and then go on to heaven. This teaching enabled the medieval church to

---

18. The original language of the Comfortable Words has been modernized. For the final version of Cranmer's Comfortable Words as found in the 1549 and 1552 Book of Common Prayer, see Joseph Ketley, ed., *The Two Liturgies . . . in the Reign of King Edward the Sixth* (Cambridge: Parker Society, 1844), 91, 276.

19. Ibid., 187.

continue to insist that every Christian had to do strict penance for every sin committed and, at the same time, to proclaim that no earthly sinner remained beyond the hope of redemption. Consequently, those undergoing punishments in Dante's *Purgatory* were in fact joyful, cheered by their now-certain knowledge of eventual salvation.

However, by the fifteenth century this pastoral safety valve permitting deathbed conversions seemed to many in the church to have become too successful. Many people seemed to be putting off serious repentance until the end because of the hope offered by purgatory. The church responded with Bridget of Sweden's much darker visions of extremely painful punishments. Eventually, purgatory as a place to be deeply feared dominated popular preaching and perception. Here is a brief portion of the fearful fate she saw reserved in purgatory for those guilty of lying pride:

> Then I thought that there was a band bound about his head so fast and sore that the forehead and the back of the head met together. The eyes were hanging on the cheeks; the ears as they had been burned with fire; the brains burst out at the nostrils and his ears; the tongue hanging out, and the teeth were slammed together; the bones in the arms were broken and withered as a rope.

Be assured, the remaining parts of the sinner's body fared no better.[20]

With such visions of exacting retribution for each human frailty, Duffy had to admit again that the omnipresent threat of terror "must have seemed at times oppressive." The "whole machinery of late medieval piety was designed to shield the soul from Christ's doomsday anger."[21] Here was the root of Taverner's and Bale's complaint against forced obedience through fear of violence. The

---

20. Eamon Duffy, *The Stripping of the Altars: Traditional Religion in England 1400–1580* (New Haven, CT: Yale University Press, 1992), 338–39.

21. Ibid., 309.

bishops were merely acting, in their day, how Christ their master was painted as acting toward all wrongdoers at the end of days. The medieval answer to the wrath of Christ was the kindly intercession of Mary and the saints, as well as the hope of saving grace through the priest during the sacrament of penance.[22] For the English Reformers, however, the gospel was not what others did to help sinners get right with Christ. The answer to the human condition was what Christ had done, was doing, and would do to restore sinners to himself. According to Reformation Anglicanism, the English people needed to understand first and foremost that Christ was the Good Shepherd. He allured back his lost sheep by the power of his self-sacrificing love.

Naturally, then, Cranmer's Comfortable Words do not begin with God's wrath. In fact, they do not begin with God at all. Rather, the first Scripture verse begins with a hurting humanity—its felt needs, its longing for wholeness. The Comfortable Words begin with Matthew 11:28.

"Come to me all that travail, and are heavy laden, and I shall refresh you." Human misery caused by captivity to the destructive power of sin was a favorite theme of the English Reformers. They wholeheartedly agreed with Luther's teaching that the human heart cannot, of itself, free itself from slavery to sin and selfishness. Listen to what the second sermon from the Book of Homilies says. Entitled "The Misery of All Mankind," it concisely sums up sin's effect on human nature: "We are sheep that run astray, but we cannot of our own power come again to the sheepfold, so great is our imperfection and weakness."[23] Because of their "feeling faith," the Reformers' understanding of human nature was rooted in their own deeply entrenched soul sickness. In fact, Cranmer appears to have chosen the word "travail" instead of the more usual "labor"

---

22. Ibid., 187–88, 310.

23. Ronald B. Bond, *Certain Sermons or Homilies (1547) and A Homily against Disobedience and Wilful Rebellion (1570): A Critical Edition* (Toronto: University of London Press, 1987), 74.

specifically because of its inclusion of emotional, not merely physical, weariness.

Of course, it was precisely because of their penetrating inner woundedness that the graciously gentle gospel of the Reformation seemed good news to the first English Protestants. Katherine mentioned, in particular, the alluring power of Jesus's offer in Matthew 11:28 to meet her at the point of her need. Cranmer gave an enduring voice to these spiritual anxieties in his confession in the 1549 Book of Common Prayer: "Almighty God, Father of our Lord Jesus Christ, maker of all things, judge of all men, we acknowledge and bewail our manifold sins and wickedness . . . : the remembrance of them is grievous unto us, the burden of them is intolerable."

Slavery to selfish acts and the innate sense of guilt that resulted—here were the two fundamental sources for human misery. What could be done about them? For the English Reformers, the answer lay in divine action alone. We can see this in the absolution that followed the confession. The minister asked God to "pardon and deliver" the congregation. Why two verbs instead of merely one? Because Cranmer was making clear that humanity needed to turn to God as the only antidote for both sources of human misery. Only God could heal a conscience wounded by selfish acts.[24] Only God could set free a will chained to self-centeredness.

In the 1552 prayer book, Cranmer reinforced these themes by adding a new opening for the daily office, which once again compared sin-sick humanity to helpless sheep:

> Almighty and most merciful Father, we have erred and strayed from your ways, like lost sheep. We have followed too much the devices and desires of our own hearts. We have offended against your holy laws. We have left undone those things which we ought to have done, and we have done those things which we ought not to have done, and there is no health in us.[25]

---

24. Ketley, *Liturgies of Edward the Sixth*, 6–7, 90–91 (the English has been modernized for all quotations from this text).

25. Ibid., 218–19.

Now both Morning and Evening Prayer began with a confession of humanity's profound spiritual neediness in the face of its ongoing struggle with self-centered waywardness. As a result, Cranmer made the essence of Anglican worship turning to God because of sin so as to be turned by God from sin.

"God so loved the world, that he gave his only begotten Son to the end that all that believe in him, should not perish, but have everlasting life." Having used Jesus's own words to acknowledge the depth of human longing for good news, Cranmer's second Comfortable Word now turns again to Jesus to establish the depth of God's own longing to respond. The divine desire and initiative to save his people is at the very heart of the English Reformers' theology. John 3:16 makes clear that God the Father, moved by the love which is his very being, sent God the Son into this world to become the visible embodiment of the divine Good Shepherd. Jesus came to seek out the lost, gently freeing lambs caught in the thicket of sin. He laid down his own life so that in the end he could bear his wandering creatures safely back to the flock on his own wounded shoulders. In the face of such alluring love, the Reformers were convinced, even the sin-sodden souls of humanity could not but find themselves drawn by their own inner longings back to their Creator.

Of course, the medieval church read John 3:16 too. In fact, the typical English depiction of Jesus as coming Judge had him displaying his wounds and the instruments of the torture he suffered on their behalf.[26] Yet this depiction of divine love was not intended to be a means of wooing humanity back to the fold. Rather, the reminder of Christ's passion was to render them without excuse if they had failed to repent. In effect, the medieval church said to Christians, "Here, look at what Jesus did for you. What have you done for him lately?" Because of that "moralistic strain," noted by Duffy, the medieval church expected Christians to sweat to prove

---

26. Duffy, *The Stripping of the Altars*, 157.

themselves worthy of the divine love that had been in so costly a way lavished on them.

Nothing could have been further from the Reformers' understanding. Here is the truly revolutionary nature of the gospel they found in Scripture. The red thread that runs throughout Cranmer's writings is this simple truth: the glory of God is to love the unworthy. For the early English Protestants, nothing established that principle as clearly as God's decision not to base salvation on personal merit, not even on the kind of grace-assisted human choices that the King's Book insisted was the true interpretation of Augustine.[27] No, personal belief brought about salvation, as John 3:16 suggested, rather than personal accomplishment. Eternal life with God came through simply trusting his saving acts on humanity's behalf, rather than one's own. In short, by faith sinners were adopted into God's family forever. They no longer had to fear that they were merely foster children living under the constant threat of being disowned as the Devil's in the face of every fresh case of disobedience.

"Hear also what Saint Paul says. This is a true saying, and worthy of all men to be received, that Jesus Christ came into the world to save sinners."[28] Having laid out the two sides—the longing of humanity for relief and the longing of God to rescue—Cranmer, in his third Comfortable Word, circles back like a hawk to the human condition, but now at a higher level. On the one hand, humanity's situation is described no longer in subjective terms of felt needs but rather as the objective consequences of violating divine law. Humanity suffers from spiritual fatigue because that is merely the most readily apparent fruit of human sinfulness. As rebels against divine order, people are cut off from God's peace now and stand under the threat

---

27. T. A. Lacey, *The King's Book* (London: SPCK, 1932), 147–51; and for the comment about Augustine, ibid., 149.

28. The 1548 version of "The Order for the Administration of the Lord's Supper or Holy Communion" had "worthy of all men to be embraced and received" (Ketley, *Liturgies of Edward the Sixth*, 7).

of the divine wrath to come. Humanity's refreshment can only come by addressing human sin. On the other hand, to do so is also clearly beyond human beings. Having been so weakened by sin's power, they cannot cooperate with grace to achieve their salvation. According to Cranmer, that would be the "ready way unto desperation."[29] First Timothy 1:15 makes plain that here is the reason Jesus came into this world. It is Christ's mission to save sinners, not their own. As Cranmer's "Homily of Salvation" expressed it:

> Justification is not the office of man, but of God. For man cannot justify himself by his own works neither in part nor in the whole. . . . But justification is the office of God only, and is not a thing which we render unto him, but which we receive of him, not which we give to him, but which we take of him, by his free mercy, and by the only merits of his most dearly beloved Son.[30]

Only upon realizing this distinction did Bilney and the other English Reformers find refreshment from their spiritual fatigue.

"Hear also what Saint John says. If any man sin, we have an advocate with the father, Jesus Christ the righteous, and he is the propitiation for our sins." With the fourth Comfortable Word we have come full circle. In I Timothy 1:15, the gospel truth about the human condition was seen from the human point of view: How can I be saved? Now we turn to the gospel truth about the human condition from God's prospective: How can God be true to both his righteous nature and his enduring love for an unrighteous humanity? First John 2:1–2 concisely states that problem from heaven's point of view. God's justice requires "propitiation," that is, the fulfilling of his determination to destroy sin because of all the hurt and harm it causes. Of course, Cranmer's confession for Communion explicitly acknowledged the need for such propitiation, saying that the congregation had sinned "by thought, word, and deed, against

---

29. Cox, *Miscellaneous Writings and Letters of Thomas Cranmer*, 94.
30. Ibid., 131.

thy divine majesty, provoking most justly thy wrath and indignation against us."[31] That's why the only answer to human misery
was utter divine graciousness, God's taking humanity's sin upon
himself so he can destroy sin on the cross without having to destroy
humanity as well. Cranmer's eucharistic prayer clearly affirmed the
complete effectiveness of Christ's death to take away God's wrath.
The cross was "a full, perfect and sufficient sacrifice, oblation and
satisfaction, for the sins of the whole world."[32] As a result, according
to the "Homily on Salvation," "the justice of God and his mercy did
embrace together and fulfilled the mystery of our redemption."[33]
What good news! As 1 John 2:1–2 reminds us, because Christ has
made the sacrifice that has removed God's wrath from us, he now is
our advocate. Jesus himself is the one who stands by our side. He is
the one who answers for us when we are accused of being sinners!
Here is the heart of the revolution in understanding of Jesus that
the English Reformers wanted to proclaim. Jesus is not our Judge.
He is our defense lawyer.

Yet, there is still more to the story. John's use of legal language
reinforced the Reformers' understanding of how people can have a
right relationship with God. The theological term for that is *justification*, that is, "just as if I had never sinned." Protestants believe
that this theological word should be understood in the legal sense of
being "declared righteous." That's what the Greek word for *justification* means; *dikaiōsis* is used specifically of what a judge does in a
courtroom, acquitting defendants of charges by declaring them "not
guilty." Of course, the medieval church used Latin, and the Latin
term for *justification* means "to be made righteous." That's why
the medieval church argued that the moment someone had sinned,
they no longer had a relationship with God. In the medieval view,
only the perfectly righteous were justified—good enough to have a
relationship with God. Once they sinned, they lost their salvation

---

31. Ibid., 6.
32. Ibid., 88.
33. Ibid., 129.

until they did penance to become good enough again to get back in with God.

The New Testament was written in Greek, so it made perfect sense to the English Reformers to follow the Greek understanding of the word rather than the later Latin one. Consequently, for Protestants, believers can have an ongoing relationship with God even though we are not totally freed from sin and selfishness in this life. When we trust Jesus to win divine forgiveness for us, he will act as our advocate. He will present the cross as the answer to the charges that we are not good enough for God. Then God the Father, as Judge, will accept Jesus's righteousness as the best possible and indeed the only possible defense on our behalf. As Cranmer's confession for Holy Communion expressed it: "For thy Son our Lord Jesus Christ's sake, forgive us all that is past."[34] Because of Jesus, God the Father declares us "not guilty" of any sin which would separate us from him. Thus, Cranmer concluded his four promises of the gospel as he had begun, with utter reliance on Christ's saving activity both to meet human needs and to fulfill divine desires.

"Lift Up Your Hearts"

With Cranmer's four Comfortable Words we have Reformation Anglicanism's gospel of transforming grace. Here also is his understanding of apostolic succession. Cranmer did not believe that the apostles passed down the Holy Spirit through an unbroken pipeline of holy bishops. No, for Cranmer, the author of the founding formularies of Anglicanism, apostolic succession meant the passing down of apostolic teaching. Christian faith and morals had been divinely revealed and recorded in the Bible. Its saving truths were unalterable. Each generation of the church was to receive, witness to, and pass on the Bible and its message of salvation by grace alone through faith alone. As each generation proclaimed this timeless gospel through Word and sacrament, the Holy Spirit would go forth

---

34. Ketley, *Liturgies of Edward the Sixth*, 91.

afresh into the lives of that era, changing hearts, moving wills, and inspiring people to love and serve God and their neighbors.

If the message of transforming grace was to be unchanging, what about the packaging? As a Renaissance humanist like Erasmus, Cranmer believed that every presentation of a message had to be tailored to the needs of its specific audience. How else could the audience be allured to embrace the message unless the manner of the presentation took into account what would move them? Consequently, Cranmer taught that the church's presentation of the gospel had to evolve and change as the society it addressed did. If the church did not, how could it have any hope of continuing to reach its audience, generation after generation? Liturgy had to proclaim the good news in the light of the current needs and aspirations of the people. In short, for Cranmer the gospel message had to be unchanging, but its presentation equally had to be constantly adapting.

The technical terms for Cranmer's distinction are the *regulative* versus the *normative* use of Scripture. For the English Reformers, the Bible was regulative in matters of faith and morals. The church had to have a *specific biblical teaching or rule* to say a Christian had to believe and act in a certain way to be saved. If a teaching or behavior was not directly stated in Scripture, the church could not say it was required for salvation. However, in matters of presenting the gospel, like worship and church structure, the church was free to adapt this "packaging" to the local needs of the current audience, so long as nothing they devised contradicted the Bible. Scripture was the *normal standard* of what was acceptable. If an effective packaging of the gospel for one generation made it difficult for a later generation to hear its message, then the packaging needed to be changed, so long as it stayed true to the biblical message.

Cranmer had a sharp disagreement with John Knox and the more aggressive of the later Puritans on this issue. Knox and his followers believed that everything a person did in every aspect of life had to have a clear biblical command. And what was true of individuals was, of course, especially true for the church. Knox demanded an unchanging, uniform packaging of the gospel across all times and places according to the regulative principle. In the end, Cranmer's view was adopted as Article 34 of the Thirty-Nine Articles:

> It is not necessary that traditions and ceremonies be in all places one, or utterly like; for at all times they have been diverse, and may be changed according to the diversities of countries, times, and men's manners, so that nothing be ordained against God's Word. . . . Every particular or national Church has authority to ordain, change, and abolish, ceremonies or rites of the Church ordained only by man's authority, so that all things be done to edifying.[35]

Of course we have already seen this missionary strategy at work. The English Reformers held head and heart together in their proclamation of the gospel to be true to the needs of their audience. Although worshiping in Latin rather than Greek had made sense in ancient Rome, it was equally true that worshiping in contemporary English rather than Latin now made sense in sixteenth-century England. If the medieval English church presented Jesus as a keen-eyed hawk scanning the flock to be sure to punish the slightest sin, Protestant preachers first had to seek to allure their people back to God with the good news of Jesus's genuine, gentle concern for humanity's own inner longings. Only then could they begin to lead their congregations gradually to greater doctrinal understanding. Clearly, all these themes came together in Cranmer's Comfortable Words. Nevertheless, they found their fullest expression in Cranmer's final placement of them at the very center of the church's greatest form of divine allurement—Holy Communion.

In keeping with his understanding of apostolic succession, Cranmer's "Homily on Scripture" plainly taught that the Bible was a

---

35. Charles Hardwick, *A History of the Articles of Religion* (Cambridge: Deighton Bell, 1859), 295. Note that the first section is from Cranmer's Forty-Two Articles, and the second part was an Elizabethan addition which reinforced Cranmer's view.

divine instrument by which God turned his people to himself: "The words of Holy Scripture . . . have power to convert through God's promise, and they be effectual through God's assistance . . . they have ever a heavenly spiritual working in them."[36] In the 1552 version of his Communion service, Cranmer decided to make the fresh proclamation of the gospel the immediate supernatural means by which God drew his people toward a direct encounter with him in the sacrament. When on trial for his life because of his views of the Eucharist, Cranmer made clear that he took literally the priest's words "Lift up your hearts!"

> We should consider, not what the bread and wine be in their own nature, but what they import to us and signify . . . that lifting up our minds, we should look up to the blood of Christ with our faith, should touch him with our mind, and receive him with our inward man; and that, being like eagles in this life, we should fly up into heaven in our hearts, where that Lamb is resident at the right hand of his Father . . . by whose passion we are filled at his table.[37]

Consequently, he revised the liturgy so that the priest said the four gospel sentences immediately before asking the people to lift up their hearts. Now the Comfortable Words became God's divine instrument to allure believers to seek union with Christ and each other in heavenly places.

Here is the hallmark of Reformation Anglicanism's gospel of transforming grace. The divine unconditional love made known in these four Scripture verses is intended to inspire our hearts and minds to long for communion with the living God so that he can gradually restore his image in us. Nothing better expresses the English Reformers' understanding of *sola gratia*.

---

36. Bond, *Certain Sermons or Homilies*, 62.
37. John E. Cox, ed., *Writings and Disputations of Thomas Cranmer on the Lord's Supper* (Cambridge: Parker Society, 1844), 398.

CHAPTER 5

Sola Fide

Michael Jensen

In a world in which practically everyone claims to be "spiritual," the notion of faith is badly confused. *Faith* is usually used to indicate either a sort of virtue that only a few people possess ("I wish I had your faith") or an assent to propositions for which there is no proof ("blind faith").

At the very heartbeat of the theology of the English Reformation of the sixteenth century was the idea that a Christian is justified—counted right with God—*sola fide*: "by faith alone." As we shall see, this slogan was not merely a doctrinal nicety cooked up by scholars. It was, the evangelical Reformers insisted, the very essence of the Christian life itself. It was a truth that brought them and many others the comfort and hope for which they had longed and yet, at the same time, a proposition for which many would be prepared to die. It was not an accident, then, that the Anglican Reformers placed it in the center of the documents of the newly independent Church of England. As the church sought to distinguish its theological convictions from those of the Church of Rome from which it had so recently separated, the doctrine of justification *by faith alone* was at the forefront.

But for many, the taint of controversy has clung to Reformation doctrines; and the placing of too great an emphasis on them seems unappetizing to latter-day Christians—not the least, Anglicans. The doctrine of justification no longer seems to occupy the place in Anglican theology and spirituality that it once did. My purpose here, like that of other essays in this book, is first to revisit a doctrine that lies at the very foundation of the Reformation-era Church of England—in this case, *sola fide*—but, second, to consider why this doctrine, which mattered so much then, matters at least as much today.

A Sinner's Lament

There is no better example of what *sola fide* meant for the Christian life than that of Katherine Parr. She was the survivor among Henry VIII's six queens, having married him in July 1543. She was an accomplished writer, and less than five years later, when her Protestant stepson Edward VI was on the throne, she wrote a spiritual autobiography called *The Lamentation of a Sinner*.[1]

At one level, Queen Katherine maintains a dignified privacy even as she confesses her sins. There is no airing of her dirty laundry or wallowing in her misdeeds. Nothing here would provoke tabloid frenzy. But the queen earnestly laments the state of her soul before she came to understand the true nature of the gospel of Jesus Christ. Her diagnosis of her spiritual condition prior to her conversion is most grave. It is not merely that she was a sinner: in one sense, she is able to confess that she is "not like other men," and not an "adulterer, nor fornicator, and so forth."[2]

But for Katherine it was her spiritual pride that was at the dark heart of her former life. In this attitude of high-handedness, she was guilty of "most presumptuously thinking nothing of Christ crucified" and, she adds, "went about to set forth mine own

---

1. Katherine Parr, *The Lamentation of a Sinner* (London: Whitchurch, 1547).
2. Ibid., [A5]v.

righteousness."[3] What's more, "the blood of Christ was not reputed by me sufficient for to wash me from the filth of my sins . . . but I sought for such riffraff as the bishop of Rome hath planted in his tyranny and kingdom, trusting with great confidence by the virtue and holiness of them, to receive full remission of my sins."[4]

The solution to this pride was not to display a greater humility—as if to find a virtue to outweigh it. For one thing, Katherine remembers herself as being blind to her spiritual state: "If any man had said I had been without Christ, I would have stiffly withstood the same; and yet I never knew Christ nor wherefore He came."[5]

Rather it was an encounter with the cross of Jesus Christ that led to her change of heart. The cross at once revealed to her the love of God *and* her own sinfulness. It produced in her a new kind of faith: not a "history faith" but now a "lively faith."[6] What did Katherine mean by the distinction? She writes of rejecting "a dead human, historical faith, gotten by human industry," in favor of "a supernal lively faith, which worketh by charity." One kind of faith might rightly be called a virtue in that it is attained by human effort. But the faith that enlivens and justifies is "supernal": it comes from a supernatural source. After all, to trust someone else, we first need to know whether that person is trustworthy. We won't trust a stranger, not because we don't have the willpower to trust, but because we don't know if it is wise to trust someone unknown to us. But how can we know God? By our own efforts? Can we by sheer determination and effort leap the gulf between ourselves, finite creatures with limited perspective, and God Almighty, our infinite Creator? By no means! We can come to know who God is only by his self-revelation through the cross. Therefore, it is by God's own gift of the Spirit, working through his Word, that Christians come to any knowledge of him. Now, to know God is to know that he is trustworthy, and to know that he is trustworthy is to fall deeply in love with someone so

---

3. Ibid.
4. Ibid., [A4]v–[A5]r.
5. Ibid., [A7]v.
6. Ibid., [B4]r.

loving to us. That is why Katherine insists that saving faith always
makes itself known in loving actions toward God and neighbor.

Since faith and the love that it births are but the fruit of the
Spirit working through God's self-revelation in our hearts, even our
faith cannot be considered an effort on our part which earns merit
before God. As Katherine writes:

> Yet we may not impute to the worthiness of faith or works, our
> justification before God: but ascribe and give the worthiness of
> it, wholly to the merits of Christ's passion, and refer and attri-
> bute the knowledge and perceiving thereof only to faith: whose
> very true only property, is to take, apprehend and hold fast the
> promises of God's mercy, the which makes us righteous: and to
> cause me continually to hope for the same mercy and in love to
> work all manner of ways allowed in the Scripture that I may be
> thankful for the same.[7]

What we have in this remarkable document, written by arguably
the most powerful woman in the kingdom of England, is a confident
and joyful testimony to the Reformation doctrine of justification by
faith alone. It reveals not only the doctrine but also the *spirituality*
of faith alone. The three key elements of the idea of justification
sola fide are here. First, the queen speaks of the depths of her sin,
which left her powerless to please God and in dire expectation of
his wrath. Even her inner dispositions and desires are infected by
sin. Second, Katherine's call to a constant meditation on the cross
of Christ as the "cunningest lesson in divinity" reveals what is at the
heart of the evangelical doctrine: on the cross, Christ merited for
sinners the righteousness of God.[8] Third is her response. Katherine
relates the means by which she has come to share in Christ's righteousness: a saving faith, which is not a kind of worthy, meritorious
virtue but is a simple dependence on God and his promises.

Although certainly part of the Edwardian regime's campaign to

7. Ibid., [B4].
8. Ibid., [A5]v.

convert the people of England to Protestant theology, Katherine's approach was very unusual. Her book was neither an official church document nor even a statement of faith of some kind. She presented the importance of justification by faith in a conversational manner, a woman simply telling her story. As she searched the Scriptures for herself, she came to a new understanding of how to relate to God, which changed her life. Consequently, her personal testimony offers key evidence that the Reformation teaching on justification was not a piece of arcane theology, or a mere pretext for the church of Edward VI to continue the English separation from Rome. This doctrine was a deeply held conviction, a transforming truth which had the power to captivate people and to give them an entirely new self-understanding.

The Beginnings

The Reformation teaching of justification *sola fide* originated in Germany with Martin Luther, the Augustinian monk from Wittenberg who came to his decisive breakthrough in the course of his lectures on the Bible from 1513 to 1519. There is clear evidence that Luther's ideas had started to circulate in England—particularly the university towns—by the middle of the 1520s and had gained a number of adherents. However, since Luther had been the subject of great controversy and had been excommunicated by the pope in 1521, discussion of Lutheran theology was a rather clandestine affair in England at the time. Of course, Luther only made matters worse when he wrote a rather rude reply to Henry VIII's *Assertion of the Seven Sacraments* (1521), a book that sought to refute Luther's teaching and for which the pope awarded the king the title "Defender of the Faith." The king was even less amused with English evangelicals afterward.

Like many late-medieval theologians, Luther had been an adherent and even an exponent of a theological system called the *via moderna*. Essentially, the "modern way" was a description of how a person came to be saved, or justified, as a Christian. God had made a great pact with human beings. When they sinned following the grace of baptism, God would regard them as worthy of his gift of salvation only if they were "to do what is in them" (the Latin expression was *facere quod in se est*). If baptized persons did their level best to move away from sin in a Godward direction, God would cooperate with them in achieving their justification. But it remained a complicated journey.

After all, what kind of things would indicate that people had done "what was in them"? Well, of course, sinners were expected to make a confession to a priest, listing all their failings. They were expected to be remorseful when doing so—not just because they were afraid of divine punishment if they didn't but because they loved God so much that they grieved inwardly to have offended a God who had been so kind as to die for them. They were then to match this high sense of emotional self-punishment with an equally fervent commitment to do penances: various kinds of good works, like fasting, saying prayers such as the rosary, and giving money to charitable causes. Even though, according to the "modern way," a priest's absolution after private confession ensured that a penitent would not go to hell, sinners still had to fulfill these penances because every sin had a double consequence. Since breaking God's law offended an infinite being, every sin merited an infinite punishment—eternal damnation in hell. It was the role of absolution to remove this danger. However, every sin also did damage to the human community, and sinners, as human beings, had the ability and the obligation to do what was in them to repair this damage. Penances worked off the earthly punishments sinners owed because of their offenses to society.

For those who would die pardoned from eternal punishment yet having earthly punishment left unpaid by penance, the church invented the doctrine of purgatory to assure them they would still have the opportunity to undergo purification after this life. Originally intended to offer people hope that even deathbed confessions would save a person from hell, by the fifteenth century purgatory had become a place of terrifying punishment to be feared almost as much as hell itself. The only substantial difference between the two was that the pains of purgatory would not last forever. Indeed, people were encouraged to do all they could to shorten their time in purgatory. In addition to giving themselves to doing penances in this life, they also were to give money to charitable causes to gain "indulgences" from the church that would shorten their time spent in purgatory. Indeed, it was the selling of indulgences to help finance the building of Saint Peter's Basilica in Rome that set Martin Luther on his collision course with the pope. Another popular way to reduce time in purgatory was paying for prayers to be said for the dead during the mass. The result of this was a vast network of religious houses and special positions in churches called chantries, in which money set aside by people in their wills was used to pay monastic and local clergy to pray for the souls of the departed.

Another stream of intellectual and cultural reflection had added a new dimension to the piety of the pre-Reformation church—the movement known to historians (somewhat unhelpfully) as *humanism*. This was the movement in scholarship and art that emphasized a return to the great sources of classical learning. Coupled with this, leading humanists like the Dutch scholar Erasmus were also great moralists. Deeply trained in ancient methods of persuasion, they sought to move the emotions of the people so that they would regret their sins and truly desire to live for God instead. Nurturing such intense feelings in one's heart would complete the human side of the great pact that God had made with humanity.

We can see this emphasis in the preaching of John Fisher (1469–1535), the bishop of Rochester from 1504. Fisher was the chancellor of Cambridge University, its leading theologian, and the spiritual director of Lady Margaret Beaufort, the mother of Henry VII. Deeply impressed with Erasmus's writings, Fisher even invited him to come in 1511 and work in Cambridge, where the Dutch scholar remained for three years. We can see Fisher's own intensely emotive moralism in a series of sermons on the "penitential psalms," which he gave in

1504 to the household of the king's mother, Lady Margaret. The note Fisher strikes is a firm one: he is clear on the depths of the predicament that human beings are in on account of their sins. This much is certainly evident from the psalms themselves. The remedy that Fisher names again and again is "penance." As he says, "If we fear almighty God and do righteous penance, we can trust indeed to have his forgiveness and without doubt to be accepted by his mercy." He calls penance "the true purger of sin." If you punish yourself, that is to say, the mercy of God will surely follow.[9] For Fisher, "whenever a sinner weeps and wails heartily for his sins, he shall be saved."[10]

With its emphasis on deep inner regret, Fisher's theology had the ring of moral seriousness. He was not in the business of excusing sin. But it is quite clear that the proper response to one's sin, in Fisher's view, was a human action requiring a particular effort. The sinner in the grip of sin, he demanded, should in earnest seek to counter sin and purge it from himself by dint of penitential acts. But what could guarantee that the sinner had accomplished the cleansing of sin? Had he despised his sin with enough intensity? Had he expressed strongly enough his love for God? Had he truly done enough of what he was able? In the face of such uncertainties, how could anyone think that the goal of truly turning to God with confession on one's lips and with contrition in one's heart was possible for a creature overwhelmed by sin?

Both the scholastic theologians of the "modern way" and even some humanists like Fisher taught that the power of the sacrament of confession made up for human frailty. Sinners could trust the power of absolution, even if they couldn't be sure about the depth of their regret or love. Erasmus, however, felt that such teaching led to confession becoming merely an empty ritual where people simply went through the motions without anything affecting their emotions. He rejected an automatic understanding of the power of ab-

---

9. St. John Fisher, *Exposition of the Seven Penitential Psalms in Modern English* (San Francisco: Ignatius, 1998), 75.
   10. Ibid., 17.

solution, insisting instead on an authentic internal transformation of will and emotions. Consequently, Erasmus's biblical scholarship led him to challenge the very essence of the medieval understanding of penance. In his fresh Latin translation of the Greek New Testament, the words of Christ in Matthew 4:17—which, translated from the Vulgate, would yield "do penance"—was instead rendered, essentially, "repent." Penitence wasn't a mere matter of outward actions but was an inner attitude of the heart that had withdrawn from love of sin and moved to love of God instead. Consequently, the emphasis on external penitential acts as the precondition for salvation lost one of its primary scriptural underpinnings. But what's more, "repent" and "believe" could now be seen as connected, as part of a wholesale turning of a person toward God in expectation of forgiveness.

Yet, even as humanists like Erasmus increased the pressure on sinners to feel intense hatred for themselves and an even greater love for God, Luther showed how inevitably futile were these perfectionist aims. In light of the gospel, Luther decided that God is both far more severe and far more gracious than the medieval theology had allowed. On the one hand, the human condition is far worse than the *via moderna* understood. *Concupiscence*—a technical theological word which names the corruption of human desire itself[11]—is a selfish force active in every part of human beings: in our hearts, minds, and will. For we are motivated not only by pure reason but also by fears and desires, dreams, and drives of which we may be only dimly aware at the time. If we "do what is in us," our selfishness will lead us to think ourselves better than we are. We will refuse to see how sin corrupts not only human actions but the human will itself, that on our own we do not even *want* to serve God but merely want to use him for our own purposes. The righteous character of God stands only to condemn us if we seek to stand before him on the basis of our own virtue.

On the other hand, the grace of God is greater still: he enables sinners, "dead in their sins," to come to life by entrusting themselves

---

11. Article 9 insists that "concupiscence and lust *hath of itself the nature of sin*" (emphasis added); and that this situation maintains even in the regenerate person.

to the promise of his mercy. As Paul reminded his hearers in Romans 1:17, quoting the ancient prophet Habakkuk, "The righteous shall live by faith." Because of the ongoing presence of concupiscence in a believer's life, Christians are always sinners by God's standard of righteousness, but at the same time believers also trust Christ's promise that he has taken away their sins, given them his own righteousness in the sight of God, and indwelt them by the Holy Spirit. Therefore, Luther argued that a Christian was *simul justus et peccator*—simultaneously a sinner and in a right relationship with God. Under Cranmer's influence, Luther's teaching on justification began to make its way into the formularies of the Church of England—slowly in the 1530s under Henry VIII, but very rapidly under his son Edward VI (r. 1547–1553).

Cranmer's Doctrine of Faith and the Anglican Formularies

It was during the reign of Henry VIII's son Edward VI that the Church of England adopted unequivocal expressions of the doctrine of justification *sola fide* as its official doctrine. Without having to fear that they would offend Henry, the leading evangelicals could finally put into liturgical and doctrinal expression the faith of which they had become increasingly convinced. In 1549, the European Reformers Bucer and Fagius reported that in the realm, "the doctrine of justification is purely and soundly taught."[12] The Forty-Two Articles of 1552 declared that justification *ex sola fide Iesu Christi* (by faith alone in Jesus Christ) was a "most wholesome" teaching for Christians, but referred readers to the Book of Homilies for an explanation of what that meant. The Thirty-Nine Articles of 1571 repeated these essential points:

> *Article XI: Of the Justification of Man*
> We are accounted righteous before God, only for the merit of our Lord and Saviour Jesus Christ by faith, and not for our own

---

12. Alister E. McGrath, Iustitia Dei: *A History of the Christian Doctrine of Justification*, 3rd ed. (Cambridge: Cambridge University Press, 2005), 102.

works or deservings. Wherefore that we are justified by faith only is a most wholesome doctrine, and very full of comfort; as more largely is expressed in the Homily of Justification.

It is interesting to note the pastoral concern of the Article. As we saw in Katherine Parr's testimony, this doctrine is the wellspring of a great spiritual peace. It produces comfort, because it is the doctrine that assures the believer that her sins will not count against her because of the extraordinary mercy of God in Christ. The language "accounted righteous" is crucial here. The believer's righteousness is not inherent in her, nor is she "made" righteous. This is in keeping with the Lutheran teaching that believers were declared righteous despite the presence of concupiscence in them.

But what do the Homilies say? The "Homily on Salvation" (confusingly called "The Homily on Justification" in the Article) is traditionally held to be Cranmer's work and seeks chiefly to establish the inability of human beings to merit salvation. The merits of Christ by contrast, embraced by faith, are the sure ground for justification.

The homily takes Romans 3:21–25 for one of its key texts. What is interesting about this Pauline text is the way in which the apostle links the biblical metaphors of sacrifice, redemption, and justification. The justification of sinful human beings, then, involves the wrath-bearing sacrifice of Jesus Christ on their behalf. By his death, Jesus made "a sacrifice and satisfaction or (as it may be called) amends to his Father for our sins, to assuage his wrath and indignation conceived against us for the same."[13] Jesus's death is also the payment of a ransom—but, astonishingly, it is a ransom *paid by the one to whom it is owed*. This is how Paul can describe the justification of sinners as occurring "freely": not because it happens without the payment of a ransom or the satisfaction of God's most just wrath, but because God himself meets these conditions.

---

13. Ronald B. Bond, *Certain Sermons or Homilies (1547) and A Homily against Disobedience and Wilful Rebellion (1570): A Critical Edition* (Toronto: University of London Press, 1987), 79 (the English has been modernized in all citations from this work).

God's wrath is the reason, as the homily explains, that this redemption is so extraordinary: for in it, God shows that "with his endless mercy he joined his most upright and equal justice."[14] In justification *sola fide* we can see that the grace of God has not shut out the justice of God. Thus:

> Christ is now the righteousness of all them that truly do believe in him. He for them paid their ransom by his death. He for them fulfilled the law in his life. So that now in him and by him every true Christian man may be called a fulfiller of the law; forasmuch as that which their infirmity lacks, Christ's justice has supplied.[15]

Righteousness itself can now be ascribed to the Christian. But this is not at the expense of justice. This is not a travesty of God's own declared standard of righteousness: for Christ's fulfillment of the law in his life is extended to the believer—the one who is bound to him by faith.

Yet, as we saw with Katherine, Cranmer is clear that this faith is not so much a thing of interest in and of itself: "As great and as godly a virtue as the lively faith is, yet it puts us from itself, and remits or appoints us unto Christ, for to have only by him remission of our sins or justification."[16] This statement is directed at those who might argue in response to the evangelical teaching that faith had simply been substituted for some other virtue, such as humility or love. Isn't faith, as a virtue of its own sort, a kind of worthy trust that deserves acknowledgment from God? The homily insists rather that faith has an entirely different nature.

In the first place, lively faith is spiritual—that is, it has its origin with God. It is a gift God stirs up in us by the Holy Spirit working through Scripture. Second, faith is not something that draws attention to its own worthiness in the way a virtue might. It "puts us

---

14. Ibid., 80.
15. Ibid., 81.
16. Ibid., 84.

[away] from itself" and directs us to Christ. The shorthand slogan "justification by faith alone" can be misleading if it is interpreted to mean that faith is something that merits reward in the way a good work might. More accurately, "justification" describes what God does in Jesus Christ, whose benefits are received by means of the faith that the Holy Spirit enables. This is captured beautifully in those great verses Ephesians 2:8–9: "For by grace you have been saved through faith. And this is not your own doing; it is the gift of God, not a result of works, so that no one may boast."

In the "Homily on Salvation" and its companion piece, "A Short Declaration of the True, Lively and Christian Faith," we see a further concern addressed. The sermons anticipate the criticism that the doctrine of justification by faith alone leaves no reason for good works and may even promote moral laxness. After all, doesn't the epistle of James condemn a faith that is alone, without works?

The Homilies insist, in reply, that a true and lively faith cannot simply lie dormant. It must, of its nature, bear fruit in all manner of good works. After all, if trust in salvation births love for the Savior, then love for the Savior will move the saved to join the Savior's mission to glorify God by doing good for others. Living faith must produce godly living. Yet, the Homilies also insist that the opposite is true: that godly living can only spring from living faith. For no work can be good unless that goodness springs from a heart first declared to be good by God. With this crucial argument Cranmer dismisses the whole medieval penitential program of seeking to do good works in order to merit God's act of making a person truly good. Instead, Cranmer insists that good works earn no merit for themselves, but they are the inevitable consequence of faith in Christ's saving grace. Because trust gives birth to love, these works are done simply as a response of gratitude to grace, and not for pride's sake. Consequently, these works claim nothing for themselves but point, rather, to the work of the Holy Spirit in the Christian's life.

Throughout its various revisions (1549, 1552, 1559, and 1662), the Book of Common Prayer has served as a liturgical enactment of the doctrine of justification by faith alone. In the first instance, the statements about the depths of human sin in the confession at Morning and Evening Prayer ask members of the congregation not simply to see themselves as stray sheep who are transgressors and offenders, but even to admit that "there is no health in us." God can be approached only in this empty-handed way, where we offer nothing and depend on him entirely. Then, in this moment of extreme vulnerability, the minister pronounces the absolution, announcing to the congregation God's desire to refresh those wearied by the burden of their sins: "He pardons and absolves all them that truly repent and sincerely believe his holy Gospel."

"The Order for the Administration of the Lord's Supper or Holy Communion" likewise begins with an emphasis on the desperate plight of sinners before the holy God. The reading of each of the Ten Commandments is followed by the response "Lord, have mercy on us, and incline our hearts to keep this law"—a recognition, on the one hand, that the law is a judgment on us all and, on the other, that without the work of God *on our hearts*, we have no way of keeping it. The Prayer of Humble Access, likewise, emphasizes the unworthiness of the congregation to come to the Lord's Table; after all, "we are not worthy so much as to gather up the crumbs under thy Table." But the character of God is also on display. He is the one "whose property is always to have mercy." And that mercy is displayed, and access to the Table itself is given, through the blood of Jesus shed upon the cross, who—in the memorable words of the prayer of consecration—"made there (by his one oblation of himself once offered) a full, perfect, and sufficient sacrifice, oblation, and satisfaction, for the sins of the whole world."

One of the most significant ramifications of the doctrine of justification *sola fide* is that it relativizes the place of the various practices and rituals that had evolved in the church. The emphasis on faith meant faith *in the Word of God*. That is, the believer received what was connected to the divine by believing the evangelical Word of God in Scripture, and not through the supposed power of the sacramental system as believed by the medieval church. "The ears alone," said Martin Luther, "are the organ of the Christian," since faith comes by hearing. What's more, justification by faith undercut the church's monopoly on salvation, since the individual believer no longer needed to confess to a priest and receive his absolution. All the evangelical Reformers agreed that ecclesiastical institutions and rituals were of secondary significance at best. They disputed among themselves about how far to take this radical revision of the Christian life. Some argued that nothing should be allowed to compromise the gospel. These Reformers rejected anything they felt even remotely suggested that a human practice could cooperate with God in the justification of human souls. Others, like Cranmer, took a more relaxed stance. They were willing to accept a variety of inherited church ceremonies, so long as such things didn't cloud a sinner's absolute need to trust Christ's work on the cross rather than their own efforts. The English church in the Elizabethan era (1558–1603) was racked by internal strife over these matters—for example, the place of a distinctive clerical dress or the role that music might play in a church service. But all were agreed that these things were not of the same significance they were once thought to be.

In particular, all parties opposed any understanding of the Lord's Supper as a kind of infusion of grace that automatically conveyed a blessing on everyone who participated in it. They viewed that as putting the Holy Spirit at the beck and call of the clergy. Rather, they believed that only those whose saving faith already linked them to God would receive the Supper's spiritual benefits. Consequently, the Elizabethan church understood Holy Communion as an enactment of the gospel Word itself—making visible, with bread and wine, God's promise of salvation to sinful humanity. However, the Supper was no less supernaturally dynamic for being so because of the promise of God to act on the heart of the believer by faith. Thus, the Lord's Supper is an act of remembrance ("Take and eat this, in remembrance that Christ died for thee") but also a present moment in which the Spirit of God acts on the hearts of believers by faith ("and feed on him in thy heart by faith with thanksgiving"). That's why Cranmer called the sacrament "Holy Communion."

Sola Fide Challenged

The doctrine of justification by faith alone was certainly embedded deep into the DNA of the Reformed Church of England from the beginning. For its part, the Roman Catholic Church codified its teaching on justification at the Council of Trent (1564) in order specifically to preclude a *solafidian* interpretation. In the Elizabethan period and into the reign of Elizabeth's successor, James I, English churchmen were virtually uniform in their condemnation of Trent's view that justification stemmed from a righteousness *inherent* to the believer. Nevertheless, *sola fide* came to have its Anglican opponents, especially from the latter half of the seventeenth century onward (the period known as the Restoration). What writers such as Jeremy Taylor (1613–1667) and George Bull (1634–1710) sought was a balancing of the teaching of Paul and James. For them, justification included the passage of the Christian life—that is, sanctification and regeneration were both aspects of justification. This was justification by faith *and* works, with faith being now understood once again as a kind of work.[17]

In the nineteenth century, it was John Henry Newman (1801–1890) who renewed this opposition to justification by faith alone as an authentic expression of an Anglican doctrine of justification. His influence on subsequent Anglican identity has been profound, and so his opposition to *sola fide* is noteworthy for its impact on successive generations of Anglicans, especially in the Anglo-Catholic movement. In his 1837 *Lectures on the Doctrine of Justification*, Newman sought to chart a middle way—a *via media*, as it came to be called—between Protestant and Roman Catholic teachings on justification. But it has been oft noted that his reconstructions of

---

17. McGrath, *Iustitia Dei*, 281.

the history of thought are specious at best and are made to serve his avowedly polemical ends.[18]

Newman simply caricatured Martin Luther's position at many points. His own particular description of the doctrine of justification emphasized the present indwelling of the holy Trinity in the soul of the believer. When it comes to the role of faith, however, Newman was adamant that mere trust alone was not sufficient to justify. Works and faith together justify, though they do play different roles. This passage is typical: "As the presence of the soul changes the nature of the dust of the earth, and makes it flesh and blood, giving it a life which otherwise it could not have, so love is the modeling and harmonizing principle on which justifying faith depends, and in which it exists and acts."[19]

Whereas for the English Reformers, love was the necessary fruit of a saving faith because of gratitude for the free gift of salvation, Newman sought to bring back into Anglicanism the medieval church's view that love in a person's heart was a necessary sign of the individual's worthiness to be saved.

The significance of Newman's challenge to the doctrine of justification by faith alone within Anglicanism (the notion of an Anglican-*ism* being something of a nineteenth-century creation in any case) should not be overlooked. Since Newman insisted on confession to a priest and personal purity as necessary for justification, his teaching marks a move to a more ritualistic Christianity, on the one hand, and a more moralistic Christianity, on the other, since these must attend and assist faith. There is appeal in both, of course. The teaching of a strongly moral form of religion is attractive as a social glue. It offers a standard to which a society might aspire. A more ceremonial Christianity offers beauty, mystery, and the tangible repeated actions that seem to offer comfort to the troubled soul. Particularly since the Enlightenment, both seem to

---

18. Ibid., 296.
19. John Henry Newman, *Lectures on the Doctrine of Justification*, 3rd ed. (London: Rivingtons, 1874), 266.

offer an apologetic for Christianity that can be explained in terms of merely its usefulness for making society better.

Yet the attack on *sola fide* introduces three grave problems. In the first place, the effects of sin on the human capacity to respond to God have to be reduced in order to make space for some inherent righteousness, however negligible. Newman's understanding of justification must deny that the unconscious power of selfishness at work in us taints even our best efforts. Second, this results in a scaled-down salvation won for us by Christ on the cross, for something—however small—must be added to it. Christ's efforts on the cross will be effective only if I add my own efforts to be like him. Characteristically, then, sanctification becomes part of the longer-than-life process of justification. Lastly, the attack on *sola fide* usually rests on a false understanding of what the English Reformers meant by *faith*. Faith is redefined either as a work in and of itself (in which case, faith must be added to other virtuous works) or merely as "assent to doctrines" (in which case, faith is repudiated and even ridiculed as a hopelessly inadequate basis for justification).

A more recent (or perceived) challenge to the Reformation Anglican doctrine of justification by faith alone has come from the movement within New Testament studies known widely as the "New Perspective on Paul." One of the leading advocates for this new reading of Paul on justification is the Anglican scholar and former bishop of Durham N. T. Wright. The New Perspective argues for a revision of our understanding of Paul's thought in light of the context of first-century Judaism. Accordingly, Paul's polemic in a letter like Galatians is not against a version of medieval Catholicism, as Luther mistakenly thought, but against the ethnocentrism of Paul's fellow Jews. "The works of the law" are not so much moral deeds done to win merit with God but the specifically Jewish markers of identity: circumcision, the food laws, the temple cult, and so on. Such "boundary markers" helped keep the Jewish people separate from the pagan nations around them. Consequently, Paul's question was not Luther's "How can I be righteous before God?" It was how to overcome the barriers that prevented non-Jews from being included in God's plan of salvation: How can the Gentiles be included in the covenant that God made to establish a people for himself? For Wright, faith is not the means by which a person is saved but is rather a sign that a person has been saved, "the badge of the forgiven family."[20]

If proved, this insight dramatically shifts the context against which the traditional terms involved in the doctrine of justification have normally been understood. In the first place, it means that Paul in his famous Galatian and Roman epistles was making claims not about universal human nature and its determination to save itself by works (as Luther claimed), but rather about the specific moment in covenantal history that he was addressing in which the Jew-Gentile issue was most pressing.

Second, on Wright's view, justification is not the central doctrine it has been held to be, and many of the Reformation claims for its significance have been overstated. It is, rather, "God's eschatological definition, both future and present, of who was, in fact, a member of His people. . . . It wasn't so much about soteriology as about ecclesiology, not so much about salvation as about the church."[21]

That means that for Wright and others, justification is about who is a member of the covenant people of God, not an individual's wrestling to stand before the holy God. Faith, then, is the badge of membership in the covenant of God, since it involves the kind of trust in the promises of God exemplified by Abraham—which was "counted to him as righteousness" (as Paul says in Rom. 4:3). Being "justified by faith" means something like "becoming a member of the covenant people of God, evidenced by trusting in the promises of God."

There is not space here for a fully detailed evaluation of the New Perspective on Paul. That can already be found in a number

---

20. N. T. Wright, *What Saint Paul Really Said: Was Paul of Tarsus the Real Founder of Christianity?* (Grand Rapids, MI: Eerdmans, 1997), 129.
21. Ibid., 116.

of places.[22] The debates continue to rage in New Testament studies about the center of Paul's thought. Nevertheless, it is possible to offer the following reflections: First, the New Perspective has insisted that the theological debate be about what the Bible itself actually says, and not about competing confessions. Is this not true to the Reformation spirit? The Bible should be read in its historical context and with the New Testament understood in the light of the Old. One of the striking things about the scriptural narrative is the particularity of its strange story. It does not deliver its universal and timeless truths in a vacuum, like some philosopher's collected sayings—quite the opposite. Scripture has a universal significance *through* its particular and time-located texts with specific occasional purposes. This is especially true of Paul's writings. In particular, the New Perspective provides a corrective to a kind of ossified Lutheran position that pits the Old Testament ("law") against the New Testament ("gospel") without also stressing their interconnectedness.

Second, the New Perspective has provided a riposte to a very individualistic Protestantism and has pointed to the close relationship between the nature of the church and the nature of salvation. To be joined to God means also to become connected to his body. An individual is saved into a community. When this truth is realized, becoming a member of the people of God and being justified are two sides of the same coin. Mind you, Calvin, Luther, and Cranmer would all have agreed.

Third, a New Perspective understanding of justification by faith alone points to the problem not simply of moral pride but also of racial and ethnic presumptiveness. It is the proclamation of a gospel that transcends ethnic barriers. The Gentiles *are* admissible as part of the people of God, and not simply by the route of converting first

---

22. See D. A. Carson, Peter Thomas O'Brien, and Mark A. Seifrid, *Justification and Variegated Nomism*, 2 vols., Wissenschaftliche Untersuchungen zum Neuen Testament (Tübingen: Mohr Siebeck, 2001); Mark A. Seifrid, *Christ, Our Righteousness: Paul's Theology of Justification* (Leicester: Apollos, 2000); Stephen Westerholm, *Perspectives Old and New on Paul: The "Lutheran" Paul and His Critics* (Grand Rapids, MI: Eerdmans, 2004).

to Judaism. By faith, without any other qualifications or bloodlines, they are allowed to the table of fellowship with God and his people.

Even critics of the New Perspective admit that these points have led to a helpful recalibration of aspects of the doctrine of justification. Nevertheless, careful scholarship has shown that the Judaism of the first century was far more complex and diverse than some advocates of the New Perspective have allowed. Paul certainly *could* have been pointing to forms of Judaism that were similar in their legalism to medieval Catholicism, since such forms did exist.[23] While there are great elements of continuity between the Old and New Testaments, and between Judaism and Christianity, there are elements of discontinuity as well.

One should also remember that Wright, in his polemical style, tends to exaggerate the differences between the New Perspective and the traditional Protestant reading of Paul. Many of the claims that have been heralded as a "New Perspective" can be received as useful additions to our thinking about Paul's theology without conceding that the Reformation position was in error. Wright's insistence that the Christian gospel affirms the lordship of the risen Messiah Jesus is surely not denied by those who hold the traditional view. But the strong words that Paul speaks against false teachers in Galatia, as those who are "turning to a different gospel" (1:6; cf. 5:7–12), do not come because they are simply denying the lordship of Christ. Likewise, an emphasis on the corporate nature of our salvation need not come at the expense of the right emphasis on the individual's faith that the Reformation era rediscovered.

The New Perspective's understanding of the role of faith remains controversial. As we have seen, Wright declares faith to be a badge of belonging to the covenant—not the basis for belonging itself, but its sign. However, this present justification anticipates

---

23. It is worth noting that the "New Perspective" is the New Perspective *on Paul*, not on the New Testament. For the purposes of scholarship, this means that canonical epistles whose authorship is disputed are excluded from the range of texts considered. A theologian cannot simply eliminate a canonical text like that. Eph. 2:8–10 seems to be quite clearly speaking into a framework of works-righteousness; but writers like J. D. G. Dunn ignore it as non-Pauline.

what will be publically declared on the last day (in his words) "on the basis of the believer's entire life."[24] Is faith then really "faithful obedience," in some way deserving of merit just as the medieval church taught about a life of good works? Cranmer's formularies for the Church of England reject such an idea out of hand. Wright has denied that this is what he means, though his use of the word "basis" has confused and alarmed his critics.[25] Even if we take him at his word (which we ought to do), do we have to be forced to choose between an evidentiary role for faith and faith as an instrument of our salvation? For example, the famous verse from Habakkuk (2:4) that Paul uses in Romans 1:17 can be read both ways as "the righteous because of their faith will live" or "the righteous will have lives characterized by faith(fullness)." As Leon Morris once wrote, "The lives they live form the test of the faith that they profess."[26] As we have seen from Katherine and Cranmer, the English Reformers took this "both–and" option: saving faith brought assurance of salvation in an instant, but the gratitude for such certainty brought about a lifelong commitment to godly living.

As Alister E. McGrath writes at the end of his study of the multi-century history of *Iustitia Dei*, challenges to the doctrine of justification *sola fide* have led to its reduced place in the contemporary church.[27] A significant ecumenical statement produced in 1982, the report of the Anglican–Roman Catholic International Commission declared, "We are agreed that this is not an area where any remaining differences of theological interpretation or ecclesiological emphasis, either within or between our Communions, can justify our continuing separation." The document itself shows less evidence of addressing the issues of controversy than of sidelining them. It

---

24. Wright, *What Saint Paul Really Said*, 129.

25. See Andrew Cowan's report at the 2010 meeting of the Evangelical Theological Society, at which Wright clarified his use of the word "basis," in Justin Taylor, "What N. T. Wright Really Said," *TGC*, November 26, 2010, http://thegospelcoalition.org/blogs/justintaylor/2010/11/26/what-n-t-wright-really-said.

26. Leon Morris, *The Gospel according to John*, rev. ed. (Grand Rapids, MI: Eerdmans, 2005), 285.

27. McGrath, *Iustitia Dei*, 413.

gives the impression not so much of a resolution accomplished in the name of reconciliation, but of an unwillingness to see the disagreement as having ongoing significance.

It could be argued that the doctrine of justification has for too long meant a divisive doctrinal quibbling between churches. Furthermore, in the post-Christendom era, in which the justice of God is no longer a presupposition of human life, isn't it simply the lordship of Christ that should be the content of Anglican preaching? Is there then an ongoing place for insisting on justification *sola fide* today? The last section of this chapter seeks to address that question.

The Need for *Sola Fide* Today

We opened our discussion of *sola fide* by hearing from Queen Katherine Parr, whose account of her own conversion contained a clear description of the Reformation teaching on justification. She bore witness not simply to an intellectual change of mind but to a wholesale personal and spiritual transformation. This came through an understanding not simply of the rule of Jesus Christ but also of the manner of his saving her. "By faith alone" was a description of her *spirituality*. It had three clear aspects, each of which held deep inner significance: (1) it confronted her with the reality of her desperate plight as a sinner without hope before the final Judge; (2) it spoke of the unparalleled mercy to be found in the blood of Jesus, the crucified and risen Lord; and (3) it awakened in her a lively faith, the instrument by which she received the divine blessings of mercy and forgiveness, and the assurance that attends them—indeed, the *only* way by which she could receive them.

These three truths remain as relevant as they ever were—to a modern-day citizen of a democracy as to a sixteenth-century queen. We do not inhabit the honor/shame culture of Renaissance Europe, with its strict social ordering and its rigid pattern of manners. However, to "be someone" in a contemporary industrial economy is increasingly a matter of (apparent) merit, earned through hard work and study. Social status and wealth still today bring the illusion of having attained a higher moral standing. Alongside this performance-based "justification" there remains the status that comes from having the right origins. Likewise, condemnation swiftly falls on those who do not perform, or on those who are outsiders. In my own country, Australia, we are known for our intolerance of the unemployed as lazy (the colorful local expression is *dole bludgers*), and for our fear of foreigners, which expresses itself in our treatment of "boat people"—keeping them in internment camps rather than granting them asylum.

The transferal of these states of mind to the state of a person before the Creator is crude but common—and unfortunately perpetuated by the behavior and sometimes teaching of many Christian churches. The twin engines of performance-based identity and status-based identity drive the human social world and make it hard to imagine that the divine being is of any different mind. The "natural" order of things would seem to bolster a perception of God as the one who rewards performance and honors status; and, thus, the achiever and the insider are held to be the truly blessed.

The gospel of Jesus Christ exposes this natural theology of performance and inclusion for the idolatrous and banal sham that it is. In the first place, human beings are recalcitrant sinners whose plight is desperate. In this judgment, God does not show favoritism on the basis of ethnicity (Romans 2)—a challenge to the persistent presence of racial and ethnic exceptionalism in our world, where many people think they were simply born better than others. The great hope of men like Matthew Arnold (1822–1888) that education would prove a path to human improvement in the nineteenth century was exploded by the devastating events of the twentieth. Author Francis Spufford has argued recently:

> Peace is not the norm; peace is rare, and where we do manage to institutionalize it in a human society, it's usually because we've been intelligently pessimistic about human proclivities,

and found a way to work with the grain of them in a system of intense mutual suspicion like the U.S. Constitution, a document which assumes that absolutely everybody will be corrupt and power-hungry given half a chance.[28]

It may not be polite to say so, but he's right. He's exposed on a social scale the deceiving illusion that Queen Katherine discovered she had foolishly embraced: that a decent and moderate exterior is evidence of and even the grounds for an assurance that one is at peace with the Creator.

It is the second feature of the theology and spirituality of the Anglican Formularies that speaks powerfully to this lie. If there is something in us from which we can take the slightest degree of spiritual pride, then the obedient life, terrible death, and glorious resurrection of Jesus Christ do not have the meaning ascribed to them in the New Testament. But here we come to the heart of the Reformation Anglican theology: God, who is rich in mercy, sent his Son so that humanity might find in his faithful obedience to death on a cross the righteousness so sorely lacking in themselves and hence be accounted righteous because of the Son's efforts, not their own. By raising Christ from the dead, God reveals him to be vindicated, overturning the verdict of the cross and declaring him "with power to be the Son of God" who saves.

Jesus, who once was dead but is alive, is Lord. All other powers will bow to him, the royal Son of God. But the testimony "Jesus is Lord" is unique: it has no earthly analogy among human kings and rulers. To proclaim Jesus "Lord" is not at all the same as proclaiming the same of any other individual or force. It is on this account that the doctrine of justification *sola fide* remains of vital importance to the contemporary church. The lordship of Jesus Christ, in whom is victory, can only be understood rightly as expressed through justification by grace alone through faith alone—since in

---

28. Francis Spufford, *Unapologetic: Why Despite Everything, Christianity Can Still Make Emotional Sense* (London: Faber and Faber, 2012), 12.

his kingdom, membership is not on the basis of status, ethnicity, or performance.

This, then, is the identity of the people of God that he gathers to himself. They are not gathered in any other way or on any other basis than by the word about Jesus Christ, which exposes performance and status as hollow and instead introduces the divine mercy as the basis for inclusion. A church that loses sight of the cross as its very constitution loses its identity and becomes something else entirely. A church that forgets that the living Jesus himself bought it at the price of his own life and now has authority to rule it denies its very being. Is this not a terrible judgment on large tracts of Anglican history, in which the church stood for ethnic superiority, social inclusion and exclusion by status, and a suburban morality? Is not this message a magnificent call to preach the gospel in all the world, since the gospel of Jesus Christ is for all without exception?

And so we come to the matter of faith itself. For the evangelical Reformers, faith was in one sense everything, though it was nothing. To say that a person is justified by faith alone is chiefly a statement about the profundity of sin and the greater profundity of divine mercy. But it is also a declaration about the kind of response that this gospel, of its nature, demands. The gospel has to be believed; it cannot be received in any other way, or it would not be itself! But this fact does not make faith in and of itself a different species of *work*, a virtue that one can attain through being more spiritual. This popular understanding of faith as work is found across the Western world and has been bolstered by popular religion. This is why faith seems so alien to so many people, since it is suggestive of a sort of spiritual elitism. Katherine's biography reminds us of a truth we still need: that faith is not an attainment. It is the gift that comes from knowing the God of love as revealed through the cross.

Lastly, the message of *sola fide* needs to be recovered today because it is the true basis for the extraordinary good works that ought to accompany the gospel of Jesus Christ as its most natural fruit.

The people of God are no longer constrained by the pressures of a performance-based system; nor are they disempowered by a message of ethnic, tribal, or social exclusiveness. Even the priority and privilege of the Jews in the divine plan do not warrant a presumption before God: their election as God's people serves to bring about the inclusion of the Gentiles. The extraordinary liberty of the gospel of Jesus Christ is boundless in its possibilities for righteous action in the world. The individual released from the deadening weight of a guilty conscience, possessing now all the comforts and assurances of God's love in Jesus Christ, can turn with joyful abandon to the call to do what God would have done in the world—signifying that the faith in which the believer stands is, as Cranmer would have put it, a "lively faith."

CHAPTER 6

Soli Deo Gloria

Ben Kwashi

My glory I will not give to another. (Isa. 48:11)

So, whether you eat or drink, or whatever you do, do all to the glory of God. (1 Cor. 10:31)

Introduction

We praise you, O God, we acknowledge you to be the Lord.
All the earth does worship you: the Father everlasting. . . .
Heaven and earth are full of the Majesty of your glory.[1]

These words have stood the test of time; they have been declared by millions of voices and are attested to by the Scriptures. But are they of any real relevance today? Does the concept of the glory of

---

1. *"Te Deum,"* vv. 1, 2, and 6, in *1662 Book of Common Prayer* (Oxford: Oxford University Press), 38. The English has been modernized.

God have any effect upon lives today? Indeed, what do we mean by the "glory of God"?

Rick Warren describes the glory of God this way: "It is who God is. It is the essence of his nature, the weight of his importance, the radiance of his splendor, the demonstration of his power, and the atmosphere of his presence. God's glory is the expression of his goodness and all his other intrinsic, eternal qualities."[2] This glory is to be seen in and through the whole of creation, in the power, the beauty, the variety, the detail, the organization, the wisdom, the love, and the life of the universe: "The heavens declare the glory of God" (Ps. 19:1). God has also revealed this glory in and through the lives of his people in different times and in different places, but the supreme revelation came with Jesus Christ, who is described as "the radiance of the glory of God" (Heb. 1:3). He "became flesh and dwelt among us, and we have seen his glory, glory as of the only Son from the Father, full of grace and truth" (John 1:14).

Such glory is an intrinsic part of the nature of God, and therefore human beings cannot add to that glory; but they can (as Warren points out) recognize, honor, declare, praise, reflect, and live for the glory of God. Indeed, *soli Deo gloria* (to God alone be glory) implies that humankind seeks nothing for itself but puts everything into seeking God—not for the sake of what can be obtained from God or because a person must work hard in order to gain God's favor, but simply because humanity was created to seek—as its primary aim—God, God's glory, and God's kingdom. The focus of the whole of life and living as a Christian is thus shifted from one's self to God.

The curious thing is that when we seek things for ourselves, we may or may not obtain them, and even if we do obtain them, they satisfy us only for a time, before we move on to wanting the next thing in line, be it car, house, status, rank, job, success, or anything else. Moreover, the material things we seek for ourselves are often stolen, lost, destroyed, or thrown away; or they wear out, expire, or

---

2. Rick Warren, *The Purpose Driven Life: What on Earth Am I Here For?* (Grand Rapids, MI: Zondervan, 2002), 53.

are damaged in some way. If, however, we seek God, fix our eyes on him, seek his will in all things, and put our lives in his hands, then the Lord himself looks after us far better than we could look after ourselves. That does not mean that we are guaranteed limitless wealth, or worldly success, or even good health, but it does mean that we shall know inner joy, peace, contentment, and a purpose and fulfillment in life that would otherwise be lacking. However, the futility of seeking our own glory and the ephemeral nature of such glory are often not perceived. Many remain blind to the fact that the things of this world that we seek for ourselves last only in this world, whereas the gifts that God gives last forever, gifts such as love, peace, joy, forgiveness, and eternal life.

The Westminster Shorter Catechism states that "man's chief end is to glorify God and to enjoy him forever," but it may be asked whether this makes any sense in the twenty-first century. Why should all glory be to God? Do people really give all glory to God today? How can we be empowered truly and completely to give glory to God? This chapter tries to show that although it is widely acclaimed that glory should be given to God alone, in practice people tend to be preoccupied with seeking self-glory and self-promotion. I will delineate the danger of this self-seeking and demonstrate from biblical and contemporary examples how we today can be enabled to be true to that fundamental Reformation principle of seeking to give glory to God alone.

Seeking Our Own Glory

In the world today there is a constant bombardment of advertisements, media productions, and social pressures urging people to get more for themselves, whether material possessions, money, position, status, rank, or any other commodity or consideration. Those who comply with such advertisements and pressures, we are told, will obtain a certain glory for themselves and keep up with the competitive race for an ever-higher level on the ladder of fame, power, wealth, and social status. This is nothing new. Adam and

Eve fell into this trap and preferred to take the fruit for themselves rather than to obey God. Kings pursued their own ends—until their empires crumbled. King Herod took glory for himself and died, eaten by worms (Acts 12:20–23). Many have tried to gain a fortune for themselves, only to have it squandered by their children. The Old Testament prophets thundered for centuries against the selfish, self-seeking glory of rulers and peoples who forsook the true God and turned to idols of their own making. Despite clear predictions of disaster, few responded positively, and therefore they suffered shame, defeat, and disgrace.

> How lonely sits the city
>> that was full of people!
> How like a widow she has become,
>> she who was great among the nations!
> She who was a princess among the provinces
>> has become a slave. (Lam. 1:1)

Some have sought physical pleasure only to meet disgrace later. Others have desperately tried to win in sports, only to be stripped of everything when their drug use was discovered. Those who seek glory for themselves are often blind to the hefty price that must be paid until it is too late to reverse their own self-centered actions.

Thus, we are not surprised that, apart from the self-glorification that human beings seek in their daily pursuits, there is also a real tendency to believe that one can—at least in part—earn or contribute to one's eternal salvation. Again, this is nothing new. Prior to the Reformation, and in many theological circles since then, it was often taught that human beings could earn God's favor, if not their salvation. Cranmer, in his homily "Of Good Works," decries "papistical superstitions and abuses . . . [that] were made most high and holy things, whereby to attain to everlasting life and remission of sin."[3] As we have seen throughout this book, whether through

---

3. Thomas Cranmer, "Of Good Works," in *Book of Homilies*, ed. John Griffiths (Vancouver: Regent College Publishing, 2008), 63.

medieval pardons, indulgences, and pilgrimages or through modern self-help theories, humanity has a persistent desire to believe that each individual can earn his or her own salvation.

In Romans 3:23, however, Paul declares, "All have sinned and fall short of the glory of God." Article 10 of the Thirty-Nine Articles reminds us that man "cannot turn and prepare himself, by his own natural strength and good works, to faith and calling upon God."[4] The homily "Of the Misery of Man" states "how, of ourselves and by ourselves, we have no goodness, help, nor salvation. . . . For in ourselves, as of ourselves, we find nothing whereby we may be delivered from this miserable captivity."[5] In the well-known words of the hymn "Rock of Ages," by Augustus Toplady:

> Not the labor of my hands,
> Can fulfill Thy law's demands;
> Could my zeal no respite know,
> Could my tears forever flow,
> All for sin could not atone;
> Thou must save, and Thou alone.
>
> Nothing in my hand I bring,
> Simply to the cross I cling.
> Naked, come to Thee for dress;
> Helpless look to Thee for grace;
> Foul, I to the fountain fly;
> Wash me, Savior, or I die.

When the apostles answered Jesus's call, they began a journey that would teach them not to seek or try to get anything for themselves. Peter, Andrew, James, and John turned their backs on the income generated by fishing, gave up the stability of a family home with daily food and comforts assured, and set off on the road with Jesus. When Peter later asked Jesus what would happen to those who had left everything to follow him, Jesus replied:

---

4. *1662 Book of Common Prayer*, 566.
5. Cranmer, "Of the Misery of Man," in Griffiths, *Book of Homilies*, 21.

> Truly, I say to you, there is no one who has left house or broth-
> ers or sisters or mother or father or children or lands, for my
> sake and for the gospel, who will not receive a hundredfold now
> in this time, houses and brothers and sisters and mothers and
> children and lands, with persecutions, and in the age to come
> eternal life. (Mark 10:29–30)

Matthew's Gospel omits the words "with persecutions," but in today's world it is better to take note of them from the outset. Jesus
did not promise that following him would be easy, trouble-free, and
profitable, but he did promise his presence to his followers. At the
end of the age, those who have given up everything to follow the
Lord will be given far more than they could dream of, whereas those
who seek only to gain everything for themselves in this world will
be the ultimate losers.

Seeking our own glory, therefore, may well bring transient pleasure but, in the long term, brings disappointment, disgrace, or failure; in terms of gaining eternal life, it is a nonstarter. If the journey
of life extends beyond the grave, seeking the glory of humanity is not
a detour but rather a dead end. Those who seek to give God all the
glory will ultimately join the Lord in glory and rejoice with unutter-
able joy. This is a paradox, but if we consider it carefully, we shall
see that far from being ridiculous, it is actually the key to true life.
Jesus explains this in Matthew when he says, "Whoever would save
his life will lose it, but whoever loses his life for my sake will find it"
(16:25). This kind of sacrificial life in Christ transforms individuals,
churches, and communities and brings with it light and freedom,
joy and hope into the dark corners of a desperately needy world.

Seeking God's Glory

Old Testament Teaching

In the Old Testament the Hebrew word *kabod* (translated "glory")
meant a weight, worth, or presence, and so came to mean an objective weight, worth, or value that a person had. This was particularly

applied to God. Whether or not it is acknowledged by human beings, God has an inherent glory, a glory that he will share with no one: "My glory I will not give to another" (Isa. 48:11). Therefore God's glory must be revealed by God himself when and where he chooses to do so, either in visions of glory (as with Ezekiel and in Isaiah 6) or as a sign of his presence with his people (as with the cloud over the ark in the wilderness). The full experience of this revelation of glory came to be connected with the coming of the messianic age (Isa. 11:1–9), which in the New Testament becomes the kingdom of God. The kingdom of God is not a geographical area but is the sovereign lordship of God over his people and over his creation. That lordship is proved in the power and the presence of God through which his glory is revealed.

THE EXAMPLE OF JESUS

When Jesus began his ministry in Nazareth, he announced his agenda in the synagogue by quoting from the prophet Isaiah:

> The Spirit of the Lord is upon me,
>> because he has anointed me
>> to proclaim good news to the poor.
> He has sent me to proclaim liberty to the captives
>> and recovering of sight to the blind,
>> to set at liberty those who are oppressed,
> to proclaim the year of the Lord's favor. (Luke 4:18–19)

Luke tells us that Jesus then "rolled up the scroll and gave it back to the attendant and sat down. And the eyes of all in the synagogue were fixed on him. And he began to say to them, 'Today this Scripture has been fulfilled in your hearing'" (4:20–21). Over the next three years, he was able to fulfill that agenda because his life was centered on God the Father; on doing the Father's will, not his own; and on revealing God's glory, not pursuing personal glory or fame.

When, at the start of his ministry, Jesus declared that the kingdom of God was at hand (Mark 1:15), he was proclaiming that God was breaking the power of evil, setting right the sinful state into which the world had fallen, and beginning to bring to fulfillment his original design and purpose for creation. The signs of God's rule were present in the miracles and teaching of Jesus, who is the embodiment of the kingly rule of God, the only one who has done God's will. When Jesus healed the sick and restored them to fullness of life, he revealed God's glory, and the crowds praised God (e.g., Matt. 9:1–8).

In any kingdom, the king wears the crown, and his glory is what is primarily seen. The king's most loyal and faithful messengers or officials may sometimes shine with a partial glory, but that is only a reflected glory, not their own—just as the face of Moses shone after he had been talking with God. Paul speaks of this in his second letter to the Corinthians, saying that "we all, with unveiled face, beholding the glory of the Lord, are being transformed into the same image from one degree of glory to another. For this comes from the Lord who is the Spirit" (2 Cor. 3:18). Glory is an integral part of the life of the kingdom of God, both realized now partially and expected in the future in full. The present and future elements come together in the person of Jesus Christ. On earth the perfect glory of God was seen through Christ.

John's Gospel especially emphasizes the theme of glory: glory is revealed in signs (2:11; 11:4), in answered prayer (14:13), in the work of the Paraclete (16:14), among the disciples (17:10), and especially in the death of Jesus (12:23–28; 13:31–32; 17:1–4). The suffering that Jesus endured did not negate the glory; rather, it was through the suffering that his full glory was revealed. According to John's account, Jesus and the disciples ate a meal together, then Jesus freely allowed Judas to go out into the night; he did not forbid his going, nor did he throw him out. Judas's exit was to set in motion his treachery and thereby to bring into completion the glorification of the Son of Man. When he had gone, Jesus said, "Now is the Son of Man glorified, and God is glorified in him. If God is glorified in him, God will also glorify him in himself, and glorify him at once"

(John 13:31–32). As William Temple wrote, "God is love; His glory is supremely what most displays His love; the Passion, to which by letting Judas go, the Lord has condemned Himself, is the very focus of the glory of the Son of Man—of man as God meant him to be, of the Messiah who came to restore the divine image in Him."[6]

The glory revealed in Christ is the glory of the kingdom of God, and Jesus wants his disciples to know this glory. We see this in Jesus's prayer for his people in John: "The glory that you have given me I have given to them. . . . Father, I desire that they also, whom you have given me, may be with me where I am, to see my glory that you have given me" (John 17:22, 24). Therefore, Jesus said, "But seek first the kingdom of God and his righteousness, and all these things will be added to you" (Matt. 6:33). "Seek!" Jesus urged his disciples, "You must seek!" In his parables and pictures of the kingdom of God, Jesus makes it clear that those who will find and enter the kingdom are those who proactively look for it. The kingdom of God is not a handout to be distributed to everyone regardless of his or her attitude or concern. On the one hand, no one can pay or earn his way into the kingdom, but on the other hand, everyone must actively seek it. After all, God's love is working in them to draw out a loving longing for God in response.

But how should people do that? Do we seek the kingdom of God by looking good, like God, and better than other people so as to bring glory to ourselves? Jesus himself turned humankind's self-centered ways of thinking upside down. He gave priority not to status but to service, not to gaining personal glory but to giving glory to God. Indeed it was in order to reverse the story of humankind's self-seeking "glory" that God sent his Son into the world. In his ministry, passion, and crucifixion, Jesus defeated the Devil and the power of evil because he met it head-on. He faced the very worst that the Devil could do to him, trusting the Father to use his power to vindicate him. If there had been any kind of evil that Jesus did not face, his

---

6. William Temple, *Readings in St John's Gospel* (London: Macmillan, 1940), 221.

victory would have been incomplete, and the Devil would have lived to fight another day, continuing his domination of humanity. That is why it was absolutely necessary that the Christ suffer. Yet, Christ's passion also shows us the path to glory. Jesus gave up his own power as God the Son so that, through his utter dependence on the Father in the midst of his suffering, the all-surpassing power and glory of God might be revealed to humanity. Therefore, Paul encourages us to do the same, not to rely on our own natural power, but to depend on God working through us by the Spirit to glorify himself:

> Have this mind among yourselves, which is yours in Christ Jesus, who, though he was in the form of God, did not count equality with God a thing to be grasped, but emptied himself, by taking the form of a servant, being born in the likeness of men. And being found in human form, he humbled himself by becoming obedient to the point of death, even death on a cross. Therefore God has highly exalted him and bestowed on him the name that is above every name, so that at the name of Jesus every knee should bow, in heaven and on earth and under the earth, and every tongue confess that Jesus Christ is Lord, to the glory of God the Father. (Phil. 2:5–11)

The King of kings became a servant; the Creator of the universe was killed on a cross. By following this path, Jesus Christ was exalted to the highest place, where every knee bows to him and every tongue confesses him to be *the Lord*; and even still, the glory belongs to the Father. Throughout his life on earth, Jesus constantly pointed to the Father. It was the Father's will that was to be done, the Father's power that was to accomplish it, the Father's glory that was to be revealed. As Jesus said, "I can do nothing on my own. . . . I seek not my own will but the will of him who sent me" (John 5:30).

Whether we refuse to accept for ourselves praise and glory is itself a litmus test for our Christian maturity. Jesus asked, "How can you believe, when you receive glory from one another and do not seek the glory that comes from the only God?" (John 5:44). Some of those who wanted to believe in Jesus dared not confess their faith "so that they would not be put out of the synagogue; for they loved the glory that comes from man more than the glory that comes from God" (John 12:42–43). Clearly, we cannot glorify God if we are seeking the glory of this world for ourselves.

Yet, there is another, more serious, but still easily overlooked barrier to glorifying God—trying to honor God in our own strength. In Jesus's day, those who knew that they were sinners or failures in human terms found it easier to confess their faith in Christ. Knowing their own brokenness, they had nothing to lose by risking total dependence on him, and they soon discovered that they had everything to gain! Still, we must not forget that total dependence included recognizing their inability to fully give themselves to God. As the man with the mute son said to Jesus, "I believe; help my unbelief!" (Mark 9:24). To trust fully in Jesus meant admitting his need for Jesus to help him even with his lack of total trust. Those, however, who were confident in their own faithfulness found it difficult to admit they needed God's help to serve him with all their hearts. Consider the rich young man who sadly turned back when Jesus challenged him to give away his possessions and follow him. Although outwardly the young man had progressed far in keeping the law, Jesus knew that his riches had captured his heart. The young man wasn't free to risk everything for Jesus; even worse, he couldn't admit that he needed Jesus's help to do so.

The proclamation of the kingdom is accompanied by a challenge to act, yet we can only do so when we, like Jesus, realize we cannot rely on our own strength. The Reformers understood the frailty of human resolve and the reality of mixed human motivations. That's why Cranmer's confession leads us to say, "There is no health in us." The glory of God is revealed when he empowers the broken and inner-conflicted to make the hard choices that come with following Jesus. Indeed, we shall begin to grasp his true glory only when we are allured by his goodness to rely on the Spirit to respond positively to the challenges of discipleship.

The Witness of the Church: Power and Protection

God's glory and his mission are deeply intertwined. When God reveals his glory, his people become passionate about mission. The encounters that men and women have with the revealed glory of God make them dependent, amenable, available, and ready for God to use in mission.

Having fled from Egypt as a murderer, Moses was working as a shepherd in the desert when the Lord suddenly called him (Exodus 3–4). The voice of God came from within a bush that was burning but not consumed by the fire; Moses was called to approach cautiously, for the place was "holy ground" (Ex. 3:5). In fear, Moses hid his face from the glory of God. The call, however, was insistent, personal, and for a specific mission: the Lord spoke, "I will send you to Pharaoh that you may bring my people, the children of Israel, out of Egypt" (Ex. 3:10). Faced with such a seemingly impossible task, Moses had the courage to plead with God and to offer objections to his call. In the end, however, Moses was reminded of the Lord's absolute authority and power to use him for divine purposes, and God sent him on his mission.

Centuries later, the prophet Isaiah received a great vision of the glory of God, and he responded with awe and wonder (Isa. 6:1–8). Unlike Moses, Isaiah was already in the temple listening for what God might say, but like Moses, he was all too aware of his sin and unworthiness. Yet, when God made provision for his inadequacy, he at once offered to go on God's mission. As with Moses, the revelation of God's glory and grace was the spur to mission.

Ezekiel also caught a glimpse of God's glory at the moment of his call (Ezek. 1:1–3). This glory was radiant "like the appearance of the [rain]bow that is in the cloud on the day of rain" (Ezek. 1:28); it was so overwhelming that Ezekiel fell on his face, and he had to be set on his feet before he received his commission. "Son of man," the Lord instructed Ezekiel, "I send you to the people of Israel, to nations of rebels . . ." (Ezek. 2:3). Before the glory of God, all confidence in human strength literally falls on its face, only to be raised up again in dependence on the Spirit for mission.

Yet again, John, in exile on the island of Patmos, was struck down by the glory of God, only to be called to write down the great revelation so it could be sent out to the churches (Rev. 1:9–11). The revelation of God's glory is not just so that the favored person can enjoy it and keep it to himself. Rather, God's glory humbles human pride and prepares the human heart for its true purpose— for mission.

Paul, formerly a hardened Pharisee, received such a great vision on the road to Damascus that his life was completely transformed. He came face to face with the utter worthlessness of all his efforts to please God in his own strength, and he was sent to preach the very gospel that he had tried to destroy. Like the prophets of old, he came to understand and to live out the spiritual power that accompanies the call and the revelation of God's glory: "For I am not ashamed of the gospel, for it is the power of God for salvation to everyone who believes, to the Jew first and also to the Greek. For in it the righteousness of God is revealed from faith for faith, as it is written, 'The righteous shall live by faith'" (Rom. 1:16–17).

Paul emphasizes that he is not ashamed of the gospel; rather, he is confident that this gospel has the power to change lives and even to change prevailing circumstances. Paul speaks from personal experience: he knows how a person of another faith can be totally transformed. The gospel is dynamic. Writing to the Corinthians, Paul refuses to boast of human position, achievements, or qualifications; instead he says, "If I must boast, I will boast of the things that show my weakness" (2 Cor. 11:30). This is because Paul has discovered the priceless truth of this apparent paradox not just intellectually but, even more, in the details of his daily life. He explains:

> Three times I pleaded with the Lord about this [thorn in the flesh], that it should leave me. But he said to me, "My grace is sufficient for you, for my power is made perfect in weakness."

> Therefore I will boast all the more gladly of my weaknesses, so
> that the power of Christ may rest upon me. . . . For when I am
> weak, then I am strong. (2 Cor. 12:8–10)

This power of Christ is working toward the salvation of everyone who believes. It is more than preaching, more than talking; it
is not merely an announcement of the fact that salvation will take
place one day. The gospel is itself a divine power leading to salvation; it leads to faith and action, to the restoration of lives, communities, and the environment. The power of the gospel working in
and through a believer cannot do anything less than demonstrate
the power of God against all other forces: against evil and against
the degradation of humanity and the natural world. Paul insists
that the power of the gospel enables the ministration of restoration, which brings hope, healing, life, and love to those who receive
it, ultimately revealing the glory of God. In one of his homilies,
Saint Basil the Great put it this way:

> A man glories fully and perfectly in God when he does not extol
> himself on account of his own righteousness, but knows that he
> is lacking in true righteousness, and that he is really justified by
> faith alone in Christ. Paul boasts of the fact that he despises his
> own righteousness, but seeks that righteousness by faith which
> comes through Christ, which comes from God, so that he may
> know him and the power of his resurrection and may share in
> his sufferings, becoming like him in his death, that if possible he
> may somehow attain the resurrection from the dead.[7]

To seek God's glory, therefore, does not put humankind in a ser-
vile position of weakness; but, rather, it puts us in a victorious position of freedom under the wings of God's glory, the glory of the one
"whose service is perfect freedom," as Cranmer wrote in the Collect
for Peace. All of life is to be lived to the glory of God and with total

---

7. Saint Basil the Great, "Homily 20.3," in *From the Fathers to the Churches: Daily Spiritual Readings*, ed. Brother Kenneth, CGA (London: Collins Liturgical, 1983), 257.

dependence on the power and protection of God. Over the centuries, millions have prayed using Cranmer's words:

> O Lord God, who sees that we put not our trust in anything that we do: Mercifully grant that by your power we may be defended against all adversity; through Jesus Christ our Lord.[8]

> Almighty God, who sees that we have no power of ourselves to help ourselves: Keep us both outwardly in our bodies, and inwardly in our souls; that we may be defended from all adversities which may happen to the body, and from all evil thoughts which may assault and hurt the soul; through Jesus Christ our Lord. Amen.[9]

Here is a desire to place all in God's hands in total surrender and trust. The poet T. S. Eliot describes this desire:

> A condition of complete simplicity
> (Costing not less than everything).[10]

Cranmer and the Glory of God

This empty-handedness before God lies at the very heart of the Anglican Reformation. Thomas Cranmer was convinced that the medieval church had stolen God's glory by giving humanity a role in salvation. Of course, it was completely understandable that good people should be rewarded for what they have earned. The medieval approach to salvation made logical sense. The only problem was that it was not what the New Testament taught. Cranmer, like Luther and Calvin, heard Paul teaching that God was very different from human beings. Because of his incomprehensible love, he did the very opposite of what natural justice would seem to demand. In Christ, God rewarded the guilty with free pardon. He publicly died for those who rejected

---

8. The Collect for Sexagesima, or the second Sunday before Lent, in *1662 Book of Common Prayer*.

9. The Collect for the Second Sunday in Lent, *1662 Book of Common Prayer*.

10. T. S. Eliot, "Little Gidding," sec. 5, in *Four Quartets*, in *Complete Poems and Plays of T. S. Eliot* (London: Faber, 1969), 198.

him. He did for them what they could not do. Indeed, he did for them what—apart from the wooing of his love—they would not even want him to do. Reading his New Testament, Cranmer decided that it is the glory of God to love the unworthy, the undeserving, the unacceptable. This is the red thread that runs throughout his writings.

For Cranmer, from a true understanding of God's glory flowed everything else in the Christian's life. Because the revelation of who God is in the cross is so astonishing, so unexpected, so incomprehensible, the gospel of salvation by grace alone through faith alone has the power to completely reorient a person's heart, will, and mind. No longer is life a constant striving to earn God's favor—and thus salvation—by our own efforts. We are set free from worry about the endless minutiae of rules (the passion of the Pharisees); we need not live like chickens scratching on the ground for the smallest grain of food. Instead we are free to look up and soar like eagles in the freedom of the God-given air, entrusting ourselves into his hands. At long last, we are freed from selfish concerns and can love God and others selflessly. In this freedom, God uses us as he wants and not as we think he should want. After all, we are saved in order that God's glory, not ours, may be revealed:

> Surely his salvation is near to those who fear him,
>   that his glory may dwell in our land. (Ps. 85:9)

In short, with the freedom we find in the gospel of grace, we at last can begin to love like God loves. Now, what could reflect more fully the glory of God in this worried and wearied world than that?

The Glory of God through Service

The General Thanksgiving in the Book of Common Prayer leads us clearly from acknowledging that we owe everything completely to God (including our redemption and "hope of glory"), to asking for God's grace to help us to show our gratitude and worship through the manner of life that we now lead:

Almighty God, Father of all mercies, we your unworthy servants do give you most humble and hearty thanks for all your goodness and loving kindness to us and to all men. We bless you for our creation, preservation, and all the blessings of this life; but above all, for your inestimable love in the redemption of the world by our Lord Jesus Christ, for the means of grace and for the hope of glory. And, we beseech you, give us that due sense of all your mercies, that our hearts may be sincerely thankful, and that we show forth your praise, not only with our lips but in our lives, by giving up ourselves to your service, and by walking before you in holiness and righteousness all our days; through Jesus Christ our Lord, to whom with you and the Holy Ghost be all honor and glory, world without end. Amen.

Once we arrive at the point where we accept the free gift of God's salvation and realize that we are saved by grace through faith, then we are propelled out into the world to "go in peace to love and serve the Lord." We now seek to "do good" to show kindness, love, compassion, justice, and righteousness to all others, not in order to earn our own salvation, but because that is the only way in which we can truly thank God for all that he has done for us. We do this not as mere servants wanting to earn our place but as children of God who have been saved to serve, revealing God's glory through our service and thereby bringing yet more people to praise and thank the Lord. Pride is replaced by humility as we no longer seek anything for ourselves, but seek instead the kingdom of God.

And thus we serve: "For we are his workmanship, created in Christ Jesus for good works, which God prepared beforehand, that we should walk in them" (Eph. 2:10). James emphasizes this service:

What good is it, my brothers, if someone says he has faith but does not have works? Can that faith save him? If a brother or sister is poorly clothed and lacking in daily food, and one of you says to them, 'Go in peace, be warmed and filled,' without giving them the things needed for the body, what good is that? So also faith by itself, if it does not have works, is dead. (James 2:14–17)

God is given glory when we are committed to serving others and to the transformation of our societies.

This understanding was emphasized in the sixteenth-century German Lutheran Reformation: "It is also taught among us that good works should and must be done, not that we are to rely on them to earn grace but that we may do God's will and glorify him."[11] Similarly, in England, Archbishop Cranmer writes in the "Homily on Salvation," "Our obligation is not to pass the time of this present life unfruitfully and idly (after we are baptized or justified), not caring how few good works we do to the glory of God, and to the profit of our neighbors."[12]

The gift of salvation, freely given by God and empowered by the Holy Spirit, enables us to work for the transformation of the world around us. Ashley Null comments:

> For Cranmer, the Lutheran assurance of salvation was the long-sought missing key to unlock societal transformation. In his mature view, only the promise of free salvation made possible by God's love could inspire grateful human love. . . . In short, grace produced gratitude. Gratitude birthed love. Love prompted repentance. Repentance issued forth in good works. Good works made for a better society.[13]

Assurance of salvation thus inevitably leads to service, and service to transformation. This is so because once a person experiences that transformation which God alone can bring, then that person is propelled to become God's agent of transformation in the world.

As a young man I experienced this transformation personally.

---

11. The Augsburg Confession, 20.27–28, in *The Book of Concord*, ed. Theodore G. Tappert (Philadelphia: Fortress, 1959), 45.

12. Thomas Cranmer, "Third Part of the Sermon of Salvation," in *Saving Faith* (Kingsford: Matthias Media, 1996), 15.

13. Ashley Null, "Official Tudor Homilies," in *Oxford Handbook of the Early Modern Sermon*, ed. Peter McCullough, Hugh Adlington, and Emma Rhatigan (Oxford: Oxford University Press, 2011), 348–65, at 356.

One day on the streets of Lagos I was finally caught by Christ and gave my life to him. When I returned to my room, I saw for the first time how filthy it was, and I at once set about a radical cleaning-up exercise! Any profession of faith or any so-called worship that does not issue in a changed life is fraudulent. Moreover, only a transformed person can transform his home, his church, and his community. We are converted and transformed in order that, through us, others too may be converted and transformed.

I am convinced that when God called me to be a pastor, it was not just so that I should read the prayer book, preach a few good sermons, take offerings, bury the dead, and conduct weddings and other services. To do those things is good—but that is not enough! I am fully convinced that the church itself is not merely a human organization with a proven structure and administration, impressive buildings, complex theology, and scholarship. No—God has a bigger mission for the church. He wants to use the church to transform the world through the gospel of Jesus Christ.

The Lord called me and transformed me in order that I might be a transformer. The Lord called me and trained me in ministry to go and transform communities, families, and peoples of all kinds. He called me and sent me to the church to remind its members individually and collectively of their position as agents of transformation in every field of endeavor within the society and the nation. Each and every person who has had an experience of new birth in Christ must remember this urgent call to be transformed and to be transformers. This is not a new call! It has been the call of Christ to all people at all times, from the days of the first disciples. "Be transformed," urges Paul in Romans 12:2; "present your bodies as a living sacrifice, holy and acceptable to God, which is your spiritual worship" (12:1). True worship creates transformation; and this transformation reveals God's glory.

Sadly, however, the kind of Christianity being practiced by so many today will never bring transformation and will certainly not lead anyone to salvation. Religions that target needs and promise material prosperity without demanding faith in God alone rob faith of its power when they give assurances to people without also producing repentance in them. How can anyone ever truly come to Christ without repenting and embracing change? How can anyone truly follow Jesus Christ without being transformed by him? The more a person is around Jesus, the more he or she becomes like him. Consequently, Cranmer writes in the "Homily on Faith," "Deceive not yourselves therefore, thinking that you have faith in God, or that you love God, or trust in him or fear him, when you live in sin; for then your ungodly and sinful life declares the contrary, no matter what you say or think."[14] Biblical faith that leads to salvation and guides people to heaven is the same faith that brings about a real change in life, producing a Spirit-led transformation of personal relationships, of communities, and of one's environment.

For example, in much of the world today there are churches seemingly everywhere and very many Christians, yet with little positive impact on society. All forms of slander, malice, hatred, and bitterness plague the church. Those who come to the church include leaders from the political arena, universities, the business community, the civil service, and other sectors, yet they fail to honor or glorify God in the public square; instead, the problems of society continue to increase. As one senior African church leader has said, "My continent doesn't need more Christians. It needs more disciples." Coming from this background are some who step forward for ministry, and while they may have had a genuine conversion, these supposed men of God cave in when worldly pressures become strong. This sad cycle leads the church itself to conform to the world's standards. And when the pastor conforms, the church conforms; the church's people, in their various walks of life, repeat the pastor's mistakes.

Christians must militate against all that is wrong; they must resist sin, take a stand against wickedness and evil, and enthrone

---

14. Thomas Cranmer, "Third Part of the Homily on Faith," Griffiths, *Book of Homilies*, 45.

truth every day and in every place, verifying every story or report to establish its truthfulness rather than drawing a conclusion from mere gossip. The fact that so many people join in doing wrong does not make it right. The Devil has deceived many and has caused a majority of Christians to become lukewarm, complacent, and even conformed to the patterns of the world. Students practice plagiarism and cheat in exams; workers steal monies and are corrupt in every aspect of life. There is an ongoing campaign to destroy the biblical ideal for marriage and family life, blurring the clear distinction between Christian family living and pagan family living. Sadly, the world cannot look to the church for solutions to family and marital problems. Divorce, marriage by correspondence, and long-distance family life are all being practiced by Christians as well as by non-Christians. Adultery and fornication pollute the church as well as unbelievers. There is no difference in lifestyle. In many places the environment is dirty and uncared for; injustice, oppression, deceit, and outright evil plague virtually every area of human endeavor; even in Christian schools, discipline is lacking. The glory of God recedes from view.

There is only one cure: transformation! And, of course, such transformation can only happen by God working new desires and choices in our hearts (Phil. 2:13). The test of Christian maturity is the degree of transformation. A truly mature Christian is someone transformed by the work of the Holy Spirit. A transformed Christian cares nothing for his own glory but seeks only the glory of God. Those who seek the kingdom of God spend their time, energy, and resources pursuing God's glory by making the world a better place for others. They show their love and gratitude to the Lord by serving with all their might in order to free captives, bring healing to the sick in mind and body, shelter the homeless and street children, help feed and educate the poor, care for orphans and widows, fight for justice, and resist all evil in private and public sectors, including politics, despite the shame and persecution that may follow.

By contrast, those who show little concern for the kingdom of

God often spend their time grumbling, complaining, and doing little or nothing to make things better; instead they divert their attention to those who may be judging or condemning them. Those who seek God's glory are too focused on him to care whether anyone else notices their labors. They do not trust flattery, nor do they go fishing for praise; they care little about man's approval. Men and women throughout history, having been saved by grace through faith in Jesus Christ, have invested their time in service to humanity, seeking nothing except to glorify God.

God is calling us now, collectively and individually, to be transformed by the Holy Spirit, to take a firm stand, to resist sin and wickedness, and, under the banner of the Lord Jesus Christ, to enthrone truth—that we may seek nothing but God's glory in every place in which we find ourselves. If we are truly Christians saved by grace through faith in Jesus Christ, we cannot conform to the world, but we must be God's agents of transformation in the world. God is calling us to teach righteousness and live in holiness, to institute the rule of truth and justice for all, and to promote the kingdom of God. The church has power only insofar as it exercises righteousness, holiness, truth, and justice in all things. To lose this focus would be to lose the power to be what God wants us to be.

We might be tempted to think that such single-minded focus is not for us, that a life dedicated to the glory of God alone through humility and service is a matter only for the great saints. We think of Mother Teresa of Calcutta, who possessed nothing and yet, through love, transformed the lives of the poorest of the poor in that vast city; or we remember William Wilberforce, who persisted for years against all odds and all opposition to bring an end to the slave trade in England; or we may know of Bishop Samuel Ajayi Crowther, the slave boy who became the first black bishop and whose missionary journeys up and down the Niger River brought light and transformation to hundreds of lives. The list of these great men and women of God goes on and on, but there is a far longer list of thousands of dedicated Christians, forgotten by man but well known to God. In their own generations and situations they brought life, light, and wholeness to individuals, homes, and communities.

Naturally, we are called to follow their example. In the words of the classic Anglican children's hymn "I Sing a Song of the Saints of God," by Lesbia Scott (1929):

> They lived not only in ages past,
> There are hundreds of thousands still.
> The world is bright with the joyous saints
> Who love to do Jesus' will.
> You can meet them in school, or in lanes, or at sea,
> In church, or in trains, or in shops, or at tea;
> For the saints of God are just folk like me,
>   And I mean to be one too.

We might falsely assume that those who genuinely give their lives to Christ and seek in humility to live to the glory of God must all become ordained ministers of the church. Scott's hymn is a helpful reminder of what a grievous misunderstanding it is to rely only on the clergy for mission. The church and the gospel need committed Christians present in every walk of life, including schools, hospitals, offices, markets, industry, and politics. In the world today there is much suffering, darkness, evil, and death. The only power that can overcome and transform all this is the power of the gospel. The gospel is not a static, ossified tradition but a living, powerful force, acting through the Holy Spirit. "The word of God is living and active," Hebrews reminds us, "sharper than any two-edged sword" (4:12), able to transform in ways that reach the deepest parts of our hearts. And every Christian is called and empowered by the Spirit to share the power of the gospel with those around him or her.

There are huge social concerns throughout the world, especially in the Southern Hemisphere: widows, orphans, refugees, the homeless, HIV/AIDS patients and their families, tuberculosis, and (claiming tens of thousands of lives each year) malaria and infant mortality. Caring for these is part of an overriding vision for the kingdom and for mission, but if any one of these works of compassion becomes an end in itself, then we mistakenly give glory to humanity and not to God.

The church must therefore develop specialized ministries to teach, care for, and support individuals, families, and communities in particular situations of need, leaving pastors free to concentrate on other aspects of mission and ministry. The gospel has brought us education, health care, a sense of dignity for human life, a concern for honesty in business, and so much more, but above all, the gospel has brought life, light, and hope in darkness—for this world and the next. We therefore are not prepared to compromise or trade this gospel for anything at all—not even for our very lives. All Christians are called and divinely equipped to further the gospel in whatever walk of life they find themselves.

An inward-looking church is a dying church, and we need to look outward in our own local communities, in our churches, and in the world. Our caring and our vision will be worldwide and without limit if our primary focus is not on one another, not on any particular group, and not on what we can get but, instead, on the gospel of Jesus Christ, the kingdom of God, and his glory. Without this gospel focus, believers (regardless of where they live) cannot survive. But we know we must, we can and—by the grace of God—we will press on, sustained by the prayers of the global church.

In Northern Nigeria in recent years we have witnessed the massacre of Christians; the destruction of churches, Christian businesses, and property; and the disruption of normal life—time and again. But in all this the believers have remained undaunted in their commitment to the gospel. I believe with my whole heart that there is no gospel of revenge or retaliation or vengeance, nor is there evidence of such in Scripture. The gospel of Jesus Christ is the power of God, so that whoever believes in the good news—regardless of nationality or locality—will show the fruit of that gospel in righteousness, holiness, and service. Believers will share physical and spiritual blessings in their communities through work as diverse as initiating economic development and providing healthcare. The Christian gospel does not destroy; it reveals God's glory, bringing life in all its fullness to everyone without discrimination according to race or sex, age or background.

Difficult times of persecution bring bright opportunities for the gospel of Jesus Christ to shine with God's glory amid the darkness. Now is the time for the character of the gospel and its power to characterize the life of believers. Now the gospel of reconciliation, reconstruction, and redirection must be at work. Now is an unparalleled opportunity for the Christian gospel to emerge and bring glory to God. Those who desire to glorify God in all things must be ready to go against the grain, because there is no easy way; nor is there any other way than the way of suffering and the cross. We are called to serve God in the face of hostility, persecution, and scorn. We are called to honor God where there is no apparent honor, fame, or money for ourselves. We are called to glorify God by serving the poor, the defenseless, the widows and orphans, and the oppressed. We are called to bring God glory in good times and in hard times, when living for Christ is easy and when standing for the gospel is difficult, demanding, and deadly.

The history of early missions in a country like Nigeria contains many examples of selfless commitment and sacrifice on the part of individuals and families who gave their possessions and their lives in the service of the gospel. God used them mightily, and his glory shined through them. Among the first missionaries to reach the Jos Plateau in Northern Nigeria were the Rev. John Wheeler Lloyd, a committed evangelist, who constantly went on preaching expeditions and lived for some time at the village of Per (Amper); and Dr. J. C. Fox, who built, in the nearby village of Kabwir, the first hospital in Northern Nigeria. Sadly, Lloyd died of blackwater fever at Kabwir in 1916. Dr. Fox, after a leave of absence to serve in World War I, returned to Nigeria against medical advice and died in 1919 (aged thirty-seven) at Panyam as he attempted to reach Kabwir. His older brother, the Rev. G. T. Fox, had died at Kano in 1912, aged thirty-one.

When their father, Prebendary Fox, heard that he had lost two sons on the mission field, he offered to finance another missionary who would go out to replace Dr. Fox. The faith and commitment of families such as the Foxes can only be wondered at. Their desire was simply and exclusively for the kingdom and glory of God.

Bishop Crowther faced extreme physical conditions and antagonism from pagans and hostile tribes, but his greatest problems came when the gospel became entangled with colonial expansion and the associated push for lucrative trade. A watered-down, anemic gospel is not the true gospel, and Crowther, at great cost to himself, stood firmly against any such thing. There is a constant danger of secularization when the church mirrors the local culture and leaves behind the free gift of salvation. Secularization propagates the cultural education and mores of the time as though they are the Christian good news itself. The unevangelized do not know the difference, and so they judge the Christian faith by the cultural gospel they see and experience.

In response, our focus must consistently be on the glory of God. We must continually rely on God's promise to transform us into the image of his Son, that we may be unambiguous in presenting the self-giving, sacrificial, generous, merciful, and kind God in the gospel of Christ. This same saving God transmits through his Son and by the work of the Holy Spirit such grace that enables true believers to extend his work among all people on earth.

We need to be very clear, however, not to think that our seeking the kingdom of God, our concern for the glory of God, and our consequent work for the gospel's transformation of lives and society means that we must travel to distant places before we can begin. Our search takes place where we are, in the place where God has put us. We must respond and embrace the call to new life that God is working out in our hearts and actions. Not to respond, not to grow, not to change is to respond negatively. By our response, either we stay blind to the glory of God—missing all that is good, true, righteous, holy, and beautiful, and joining Judas in the darkness—or we allow ourselves to be drawn into the love and the glory of God, so that we, in turn—sometimes without even realizing it—become channels of that glory. In this way the glory of God is spread, and the black veil of sin and darkness is driven back, for where there is light, darkness cannot exist: "The light shines in the darkness, and the darkness has not overcome it" (John 1:5). In the words of Mary E. Maxwell's hymn "How I Praise Thee" (1900):

> Channels only, blessed Master,
> But with all thy wondrous power
> Flowing through us, Thou canst use us
> Every day and every hour.

Conclusion

Seeking first the kingdom of God is the cornerstone for the revelation of God's glory through service, as we see in the life, death, and resurrection of Jesus Christ, in the lives of the apostles, and in the legacies of committed Christians throughout the ages. The glory is God's alone. Rudyard Kipling's poem *Non Nobis Domine* (1934) expresses it well:

> *Non nobis, Domine!*
> Not unto us, O Lord,
> The praise and glory be
> Of any deed or word.
> For in Thy judgment lies
> To crown or bring to naught
> All knowledge and device
> That man hath reached or wrought.
>
> And we confess our blame,
> How all too high we hold
> That noise which men call fame,
> That dross which men call gold;
> For these we undergo
> Our hot and godless days,

But in our hearts we know
Not unto us the praise.

The fact that all glory belongs to God alone also means that humankind cannot add to God's glory: God does not share his glory with any other. No human being possesses glory in his own right; therefore, no person can increase God's glory. The task for Christians is not to add more glory to God but to seek to be his instruments to reveal, in and to the world, the glory that is God's alone. We must therefore determine daily to ask God to quicken our hearts to do all to the praise and glory of the Lord. Then, by his grace, all that we do, say, and are should be pleasing to God and in accordance with his will. When this happens, other people will be able to thank God for what he has done in and through our lives.

Of course, the principle of putting God first applies to all circumstances and to all matters great and small. Such a selfless attitude must be sought from God over and over again until he has so circumcised our hearts that living for him becomes our instinctive habit. Then the services we offer in private and public sectors in the society, our policies and politics, commerce, production, and trade—indeed all business, religious, or secular affairs—will be transformed when we know that we are doing all to the glory of God alone. Such is the revolutionary nature of the gospel in our lives. When God's love as revealed on the cross has truly grabbed our hearts, it will produce in us a deliberate decision to do nothing unless it will reveal God's glory.

The church of today needs to return to its first love. It needs to remember the gospel message of divine love revealed through the mystery of the cross. Only then will the church be moved by gratitude to seek the glory of God in all things. Only then will the church be empowered to respond to the challenge it faces. Only then will the church experience the fire of the Holy Spirit that ignited the apostles, brought life out of death, birthed hope out of despair, and changed anger to love and fear to faith. Only then will the Holy

Spirit rekindle his people for his service and mission today, transforming lives, churches, communities, and nations, until

> the earth [is] filled
>> with the knowledge of the glory of the LORD
>> as the waters cover the sea. (Hab. 2:14)

Only then, indeed, shall the kingdom of God draw near, until John's great vision is fulfilled:

> Then I saw a new heaven and a new earth, for the first heaven and the first earth had passed away, and the sea was no more. And I saw the holy city, new Jerusalem, coming down out of heaven from God, prepared as a bride adorned for her husband. . . .
>
> . . . I saw no temple in the city, for its temple is the Lord God the Almighty and the Lamb. And the city has no need of sun or moon to shine on it, for the glory of God gives it light, and its lamp is the Lamb. By its light will the nations walk, and the kings of the earth will bring their glory into it, and its gates will never be shut by day—and there will be no night there. They will bring into it the glory and the honor of the nations. (Rev. 21:1–2, 22–26)

All glory belongs to God alone!

CHAPTER 7

A Manifesto for
Reformation Anglicanism

Ashley Null and John W. Yates III

Christians face enormous challenges in the twenty-first century. In the West, secularism has severely eroded the church's influence on contemporary culture. Non-scriptural ways of living are accepted as the norm. Although Western governmental support for homosexuality receives the most attention in the global media, the sexual revolution of the 1960s against biblical morality has left no area of sexual practice untouched. Pornography is a routine part of daily life. So is sex outside of marriage. And, ironically, even as homosexuals rejoice in their new legal right to get married in many countries, their heterosexual neighbors are increasingly less interested in the institution. Couples now normally live together for several years before deciding whether to make a permanent commitment in marriage. Some never do. As a result, 40 percent of American children are now born out of wedlock. Of couples who decide they are the marrying kind, easy divorce has made multiple marriages common.

Yet, all these departures from past norms in the West are merely symptoms of a more fundamental change—the arrival of postmodernism in Western intellectual life. At its most basic, this school of philosophy rejects the possibility of knowing absolute truth. There is no universal standard to guide people in understanding their humanity. Individuals must decide for themselves how to give their lives meaning and purpose. Everyone must be on this journey, and no one can tell another what is a right or wrong expression of humanity. Even human biology cannot determine a person's self-understanding. Transgendered people are encouraged to surgically change their body's sexual characteristics to match the person they feel they really are.

According to postmodern thought, those who claim to know moral truths that apply to everyone are simply imposing their ideas on others, no matter where they got them. Consequently, Christians who look to the Bible for guidance have no right to judge how someone else lives. In a society where everything is tolerated, such intolerance is absolutely intolerable. Not surprisingly, then, believers who have a biblical worldview and practice a biblical way of living are a distinct minority in the affluent societies of Western culture.

Of course, secularism is not merely a problem for the West. Its advocates are also growing in the less affluent countries of the Global South. The East African Revival, which began in 1935, changed the way Christians in that area lived. Family and community ties were strengthened, domestic violence was reduced, sanitation as well as community health improved, and the percentage of children in school increased, especially among girls. As a result, social development dramatically improved. However, the current United Nations Millennial Development Goals are usually implemented as the solution to social problems without any reference to the role of religious faith in making a vital difference to development. Despite the strong spiritual culture of the Global South, a secular approach is now preferred for modernization.

Yet, ironically, the very pervasiveness of Christian influence in many Global South cultures presents a much greater problem than secularism's current limited economic inroads. As Archbishop Ben Kwashi noted in the previous chapter, one African church leader has said, "The continent has plenty of Christian believers. What we need are more disciples." The East African Revival fundamentally changed the way people treated one another. Yet, all too often today, Africans who consider themselves Christians are just as involved as non-Christians in excessive tribalism, corruption, and other examples of social selfishness. Indeed, the great popularity of the American "prosperity gospel" throughout the Global South countries reinforces the idea that the purpose of Christianity is to make it possible to *get* rather than to *give*. Sadly, a Christian faith that has lost its power to transform lives and, therefore, communities is just as much a threat to Christianity's contemporary credibility as the challenge of secularism.

At the beginning of the twenty-first century, the Anglican Communion has been greatly shaken by a combination of both secularism in society and the lack of transformation in Christian lives. Led by the Episcopal Church in the United States, some provinces of the Anglican Communion now openly embrace nonbiblical ways of living, precisely because they argue that people cannot change deep-seated desires. The result has been to tear the fabric of our global fellowship at its deepest level. In the face of these realities, how should members of the Anglican Communion respond?

Anglicanism has a diverse history. In the sixteenth century, the church was shaped by the self-interpreting authority of Scripture. In the seventeenth century, the Bible was read through the lens of church tradition. In the eighteenth century, human reasoning was seen as the key to understanding Scripture and the world. In the nineteenth century, three different church reform movements arose, each looking back to an era in the Church of England for the roots of its own views: low church evangelicals (sixteenth), high church Anglo-Catholics (seventeenth), and broad church intellectual progressives (eighteenth). As a result of this history, we cannot speak with accuracy about *an Anglican way* to do theology and worship—only of *Anglican ways.* While those committed to the formularies of the sixteenth century must admit that many good Anglicans look to the seventeenth century and the Oxford movement for their inspiration, those high church Anglicans must equally admit that those committed to the founding theological principles of the Protestant Church of England remain authentic Anglicans as well. Yet, of the historical options open to Anglicans, the editors of this book believe that a recovery of the Anglicanism shaped by the Reformation is the best way forward. For in the providence of God, the timeless truths of its formularies directly address the contemporary needs of the church and the world. How do we characterize this way of being Anglican? In the following seven ways.

Reformation Anglicanism Is Apostolic

In an age of uncertainty, when the search for truth has been replaced with the never-ending search for one's "true self," Reformation Anglicanism is founded on the solid rock of the teaching of the apostles. As eye witnesses to the life and ministry of Jesus, the apostles proclaimed in writing what they heard with their own ears, what they saw with their own eyes, and what they touched with their own hands (1 John 1:1). Consequently, the church gathered their writings together in the New Testament to provide us with an utterly reliable guide to knowing both God and ourselves. After all, because God is by definition beyond our comprehension, we can only ever hope to know him by his own self-revelation. That is why Jesus became human: God in the flesh, God with us.

Jesus's teachings about the Old Testament and its fulfillment in his death and resurrection unlock the deepest mysteries of the universe. Because God has chosen to speak to us directly in person, we can be assured that what is recorded in Scripture is not merely our own opinions but eternal truths for all humankind. And these truths do not just tell us about the reality of who God is. They also are the key for us to understanding ourselves. Since we naturally see ourselves more highly than we really are, who better to help us get an accurate picture of what is going on inside us than the One who designed us, God himself through his Word?

The Protestant Reformation sought to recover the primacy of the apostolic witness after the doctrinal confusion of the medieval period. The Reformers made a simple, but significant, distinction. Scripture, as the witness of the apostles, had a unique authority for the faith. The writings of later church leaders could be helpful guides to the Christian life. Nevertheless, what they wrote about the Bible and the world could never be considered on the same level of authority as the teachings of the apostles. Christians should always go first to the Scriptures themselves when trying to understand the Bible. When readers encounter difficult passages, they need to examine them in the light of other parts of Scripture that are easier to understand. Only after they have studied God's Word thoroughly in this way are they then to compare their conclusions with those of other Christians through the centuries to make sure that their own interpretations are sound. For the Protestant Reformers, the Bible was its own ultimate interpreter concerning God and our relationship with him.

As Thomas Cranmer's "Homily on Scripture" pointed out, important early theologians like John Chrysostom and Augustine taught these same principles. The Reformers, who were thoroughly learned in the writings and theology of the early church fathers, were determined to do likewise. To make sure that the newly self-governing Church of England was truly an apostolic church, they adopted the principle of *sola Scriptura*. That's why we need Reformation Anglicanism in the twenty-first century. Only the wisdom of the apostolic witness, free to speak afresh to people today, can answer the deepest intellectual and spiritual longings of the postmodern world.

Reformation Anglicanism Is Catholic

In the age of the Internet, the iPhone, and the iPad, it is easy to think that the newest ideas are always the best. After all, who uses eight-tracks, cassette tapes, and even CDs, when podcasts and live streaming are readily available? But the wisdom of the soul is not like the science of technology. Christianity at its best has always looked back to the teachings of Jesus as the best source of knowing how God designed the human heart to flourish. But in an era centuries before the invention of the printing press, let alone modern mass communication, how was the church to ensure that the same biblical faith was taught everywhere in the world and in every generation? After all, soon after the apostles died, false teachers arose who claimed to have secrets that unlocked the true meaning of the Scriptures, secrets that Christ had shared with only a few, chosen followers. These false teachers even fabricated their own "apostolic writings" to support their religious ideas, such as the supposed Gospel of Thomas.

The ancient church's answer to false doctrine was to summarize biblical truth about God and humanity in the Apostles' and Nicene Creeds. Whenever and wherever Christians recited these basic statements of biblical faith, they could be sure they were confessing the divine truth revealed by Jesus Christ. Because these scriptural truths were universal, these statements of faith were called the catholic creeds because *catholicus* (Latin) and *katholikos* (Greek) meant "universal." It soon became customary that those who confessed the catholic creeds as true Christianity were also called Catholics.

Because Western Christianity has lived so long with the Protestant/Roman Catholic divide, it is easy to forget that the Protestant Reformers were still Catholics. That was the whole point of the Reformation! Both sides were simply seeking to be faithful Catholic Christians. Traditionalists of that era relied primarily on the medieval church for direction, whereas the Reformers looked back to the apostolic era instead. Because they could not agree on what it meant to be a good Catholic, their differences eventually led to the divisions we know today as Protestant and Roman Catholic. Nevertheless, we should always remember that the Reformers never saw themselves as anything other than good Catholics. They confessed what all Catholic Christians had always held to be true everywhere in the early church. Just like their Roman counterparts, the Protestant Reformers believed in the ancient creeds. Just like their Roman counterparts, the Protestant Reformers also believed in the nature of the Trinity and of Christ as taught by the first four general councils.

However, the Protestant Reformers held to the ancient Catholic teachings for different reasons than did the Romans. Looking back to the medieval period, the Roman church held to the creeds and the councils because its leadership believed these sources were just as inspired as the apostles. Therefore, whatever the bishops agreed to in council was just as authoritative as Scripture. Because of the Reformers' commitment to apostolic authority, they argued the exact opposite. The creeds and first four councils were to be believed because their statements could be "proved by most certain warrants of Holy Scripture" (Article 8 of the Thirty-Nine Articles). As for the medieval Roman church, the English Reformers explicitly declared that by leaning on the wisdom of its bishops, it had clearly erred not only in matters of moral faithfulness and devotional practice but also even in matters of salvation (Articles 9–14, 19, 22, 24). That is why Cranmer and the Church of England returned afresh to the writings of the apostles—to preserve a truly catholic apostolic church.

In the twenty-first century, some provinces in the Anglican Communion are beginning to depart from biblical truth as it has been understood in all places and at all times. Christ's divinity, salvation in his name alone, the authority of the Scriptures, and biblical standards of morality have all been questioned by some in the Anglican Communion. That's why we need a fresh movement of Reformation Anglicanism today. Only an Anglican Communion rooted in the timeless, divine wisdom of catholic apostolic Christianity can effectively counter the false hope offered by the deceitful devices and desires of the postmodern heart.

Reformation Anglicanism Is, Well, Reformational

The Protestant recovery of the early church principle of *sola Scriptura* challenged fundamental medieval assumptions about the nature of salvation. As a result, for the Reformers, to be a true Catholic meant not only to embrace the ancient creeds and councils but also to return to Saint Paul's teaching on the nature of justification. According to Paul, salvation was something Christ achieved for humanity, not something humanity achieved with Christ's help. Right standing with God was a gift that believers received in the moment they trusted Christ's promise of free forgiveness, not a reward for a lifetime of good works done with divine assistance. To make clear that justification was the result of trusting Christ's work on the cross, the Reformers taught that it was *sola fide*, by faith alone (Article 11). To make clear that this kind of justification was a free gift solely because of God's love for humanity, not a meritorious reward for human effort, the Reformers also insisted that it was *sola gratia*, by grace alone. According to Luther, the church either stood or fell on these two tenets of justification. Cranmer agreed. At the heart of his reform program for the Church of England was a fresh emphasis on the cure of souls, and at the heart of his pastoral care was the good news that because of what Christ had done for humanity on the cross, believers could have assurance of being children of God now and forever.

Therefore, Cranmer fully integrated justification *sola fide et sola gratia* into the doctrine and worship of the Church of England. His "Homily on Salvation" taught these principles to every parish in the country on a regular basis. Several of the Articles of Religion make the Protestant understanding of justification normative for Anglican doctrine (Articles 9–14, 17, 22). Moreover, the whole strategy of the Book of Common Prayer was to return divine worship back to the apostolic teaching about what God was pleased to do for humanity, not what humanity had to do to please God. Whereas the medieval mass was an offering of Christ made by the priest as an intercessor between God and the congregation, Cranmer stressed that God was the one who gave his gifts to his people during worship, rather than the other way around. During Holy Communion Christ gives himself to believers, supernaturally drawing them into a closer union with himself and with one another. In the process, the faith of the believers is strengthened, helping them to grow in godly love, which leads to godliness. In short, justification leads to sanctification, because Christ's character is better "caught than taught." The more believers are in the presence of Christ through justification, the more Christ's love "rubs off on them," making them more like him. Because this pastoral strategy was at the heart of everything Cranmer did, the core principles of the Protestant Reformation deeply shaped the life and thought of the newly independent Church of England.

That is why we need Reformation Anglicanism today. Every Sunday, in countless churches around the globe, the minister enters the pulpit and nags the congregation to do better for God. Progressive preachers will want their congregations to try harder at protecting the environment, fighting racism, and working toward economic equality. Conservative preachers will want their congregations to work harder at being godly, including taking practical steps to draw closer to God and serving their neighbors. Of course, all of these themes are explicitly commended in Scripture. Yet, according to the Reformers, these preachers are putting the cart before the horse. They emphasize what we should do to please God, not what God has promised to be pleased to do for us. Telling people what they should do does not empower them to do it. That was Cranmer's fundamental Reformation insight.

Only love can overcome the power of sin, and such love only comes from knowing the unconditional love of God revealed in Jesus's death and resurrection for us. Because God loves us, he has promised to save us, sanctify us, and preserve us in all wholeness for eternity in his presence. Only the assurance that God will love us, through good times and bad, until his love makes us truly lovely like him in the age to come—only that kind of love has the power to change who we are and how we live. Sadly, for so many people in the twenty-first century, Christianity means the opposite. They think Christians must please God so that he will love them. Of course, if people think they have to earn God's love, the fear and shame of never measuring up will only lead them to heartache and despair. In fact, many of those who are now departing from biblical faith began by trying to follow rules in order to win God's approval. But because they put the cart before the horse, they only ended up hopelessly frustrated. And preachers nagging them each week to do better were no help. So they just quit trying altogether.

Others decided there had to be a better way. But rather than looking back to the Reformation's biblical wisdom, they have looked to their own hearts. If human beings cannot follow a biblical way of life, they argue, then people need to reject certain parts of the Bible and embrace what they can do instead. That's why some Anglicans are arguing for change. They want to offer people a way out of constant fear and shame by having the church approve their nonbiblical ideas. Yet, leaping from the frying pan into the fire is no hope at all. The Anglican Communion needs to hear Cranmer's pastoral wisdom afresh today—that's the better way. We need to found our hope on God's promise to intervene in human lives and hearts, and not on our sincere but ultimately powerless good intentions to become better. We need our preachers to proclaim the gospel of grace and gratitude. We need to recover the Reformation heartbeat of catholic apostolic Anglicanism. Then the Anglican Communion will truly give God alone the glory for his work in our lives and in our world.

Reformation Anglicanism Is Mission-Focused

Outreach has been a part of the DNA of Christianity in Great Britain from its first introduction during Roman times. Heirs to this legacy, the English Reformers believed that Christ had come to proclaim a message that had the power to gather a community. As a result, the church's number one task was to call people to repentance and new life in Jesus Christ. Everything else about the church—its structure, worship, preaching, pastoral care, and outreach into the community—had to be designed to support this mission directive. We can see this strategy at work in how Cranmer guided the Protestant Reformation under Edward VI. Naturally, Cranmer's first major liturgical change was the introduction of Reformation preaching through the Book of Homilies. He wanted to stir up saving faith in the hearts and minds of the English people by having them hear the gospel message clearly presented during Sunday worship. Then, two years later Cranmer reinforced Reformation teaching with the introduction of a new prayer book. He replaced the Latin liturgy with a service in English that emphasized the power of the gospel through Word and sacrament to move people's hearts to love God and one another.

Although Cranmer's primary mission focus was the conversion of the English people, he was also concerned about the proclamation of the gospel in other outwardly Christian lands. He tried, without success, to gather a European-wide summit of Reformation theologians to foster unity on doctrine so Protestants could present a unified witness as they sought to reform churches throughout the countries in Europe. As for those outside the Continent, England would not have its first successful colonies until the seventeenth century, and with so much work needed to bring the gospel to English and European Christians, Cranmer made no effort to promote overseas missions. Yet, he did not neglect evangelizing those with no Christian background entirely. A Collect for Good Friday asked God to deliver all "Jews, Turks, Infidels, and heretics" from "contempt of thy word" in order to bring them home to the one flock of Jesus Christ.

Later Anglicans built mighty overseas mission societies on this slender Reformation foundation. They sought to glorify God by taking the gospel to the ends of the earth. In due course, the faith and practice of the Protestant Church of England gave birth to the worldwide Anglican Communion. As a result, mission for Anglicans today is actually much more like what Cranmer had envisioned during the Reformation. On the one hand, churches in each province must take responsibility for reaching their own people, both those with a Christian background and those without. On the other hand, each province should do what it can to help the other provinces in the communion with their local missionary efforts. That's what it means to be part of a worldwide church, namely, the sharing of resources for mission in each and every locale, that God might glorify himself through the service of his global family. Ironically, in the face of the challenges of secularism, many of the provinces that sent out missionaries are now themselves in need of assistance to help promote saving faith. That is why we need a fresh movement of Reformation Anglicanism today. The Anglican Communion needs to find new vigor for converting and discipling people, both those with a false understanding of the gospel and those with none—just as Cranmer did.

Reformation Anglicanism Is Episcopal

Roman Catholics believe that Jesus appointed bishops to lead the church, since they are the successors to the apostles. Bishops have been divinely entrusted with the spiritual oversight of their dioceses, and all clergy work under their authority and as an extension of the bishop's ministry. In the sixteenth century, John Calvin argued that the New Testament established a leadership team of pastors, teachers, elders (for congregational discipline), and deacons (for social welfare). Since the last two offices were to be filled by laypeople, Calvin clearly broke with the long tradition of clerical control over church life. The English Reformers, however, rejected both alternatives. Like the Lutherans, Anglicans during the Reformation believed that church structures were not permanently fixed by divine decree, but needed to be adapted to individual cultures and historical circumstances so as to support the church's mission most effectively.

For Richard Hooker, the great defender of the English Reformation under Queen Elizabeth I, Calvin's mistake was to take a church government which fit the particular needs of his local city-state at that time and fashion a universal rule for all congregations in every place and era.[1] Hooker argued that the New Testament showed two different models side by side: a college of elders at Ephesus[2] and a single bishop over elders at Jerusalem under James,[3] both appointed by the apostles.[4] However, it very quickly became clear that the team approach to leadership opened the church to factions and doctrinal deceptions; consequently, the ancient church universally adopted the episcopal form of government. According to Hooker's historical narrative, because Scripture showed more than one pattern of church governance, what ultimately mattered was which option made the church's mission most effective in the contemporary context. Since episcopacy had a scriptural basis, and the experience of the church had "found it good and requisite to be so governed,"[5] the English Reformers were right to retain the ancient church structure of bishops, priests, and deacons. For Reformation Anglicanism, even if bishops are not the *esse* (essential nature) of the church, as Roman Catholics teach, they remain the *bene esse* (essential for the well-being) of the church.

What, then, are Anglican bishops supposed to do that is so important for the church? According to Cranmer's service of consecration, a bishop's chief responsibility is to proclaim and defend the apostolic faith as taught by the Scriptures. Listen to three questions a candidate for bishop had to answer:

---

1. Richard Hooker, *Of the Laws of Ecclesiastical Polity*, in *The Folger Library Edition of the Works of Richard Hooker*, ed. Speed Hill (Cambridge, MA: Belknap, 1977), pref. 2.7; 1:9–10. The first reference uses the passage numbering system in John Keble, ed., *The Works of . . . Mr. Richard Hooker*, 7th ed., rev. R. W. Church and F. Paget (Oxford, 1888).

2. Acts 20:17–28. Note that the leaders were called both presbyters/elders (v. 17) and bishops/overseers (v. 28) in this passage.

3. Acts 12:17; 21:17–18; cf. 15:13.

4. Hooker, *Laws of Ecclesiastical Polity*, VII.5.1–2; 3:159–61.

5. Ibid., VII.5.8; 3:168.

Are you persuaded that the holy scriptures contain sufficiently all doctrine, required of necessity for eternal salvation, through the faith in Jesus Christ?

Will you then faithfully exercise yourself in the said holy scriptures, and call upon God by prayer for the true understanding of the same, so as you may be able by them to teach and exhort with wholesome doctrine, and to withstand and convince the gainsayers?

Be you ready with all faithful diligence, to banish and drive away all erroneous and strange doctrine, contrary to God's Word, and both privately and openly to call upon, and encourage others to the same?[6]

Clearly, a bishop was expected to be as vigorous in denouncing false religious notions as he was to be faithful in spreading saving truth.

Why was episcopal vigilance in safeguarding the apostolic faith so important? Because Cranmer firmly believed that Christian fellowship could only be based on a common understanding of saving faith. Listen to his prayer for Christian unity from the service of Holy Communion: "Inspire continually the universal church with the spirit of truth, unity, and concord: And grant that all they that do confess your holy name, may agree in the truth of your holy Word, and live in unity and godly love." The church whose people are shaped by the same biblical truths will learn to love one another and so live together in peace. Yet, maintaining doctrinal unity is easier said than done. As Hooker pointed out, the early church found it a perpetual challenge in every generation. That's why they adopted episcopal governance, so as to have a clear leader focused on this task with the undisputed authority to act. As in so many other matters, the English Reformers simply sought to restore the office of bishop to this, its ancient, apostolic role—the preservation of church unity by promoting and protecting the saving truths of Scripture.

---

6. Joseph Ketley, ed., *The Two Liturgies . . . in the Reign of King Edward the Sixth* (Cambridge: Parker Society, 1844), 352.

Thus, for Reformation Anglicanism, apostolic succession is not the passing of the Holy Spirit from bishop to bishop in an unbroken chain back to the apostles and then Jesus himself. According to the English Reformers, people encounter the Holy Spirit when God speaks to them through the Bible. As his Word goes forth through preaching and the administration of the sacraments, so does his breath/Spirit. Hence, true apostolic succession is the faithful passing on of apostolic saving truth from one generation to another. Although bishops have a primary responsibility to foster this transfer of scriptural wisdom, all members of the church share in this sacred task: theologians with one another, seminary professors with their students, clergy with their congregations, Sunday school teachers with their pupils, parents with their children, friends and colleagues with their peers, indeed every Christian as God gives opportunity, both with those in the church and those without. For Reformation Anglicanism, however, bishops should set the example in their own ministries and encourage all members of their flocks to do likewise, both embracing the gospel and passing it on to others.

Not all Anglican bishops today proclaim and defend apostolic truth. Nor do all Anglican provinces think that the communion needs to be held together by a common understanding of the gospel. Some suggest that a global partnership for social justice and environmental advocacy is the best way to hold on to our historic worldwide ties. Still others believe that the current institutional structures are sufficient in themselves for Anglican unity: each province simply needs to maintain its own connection to Canterbury while recognizing that all provinces have the right to make their own decisions about faith and morals. For these folks, agreeing to disagree is the true essence of Anglicanism. The national churches should just get on with Christian mission as each understands it and partner with Canterbury and other provinces as they can. Yet, as Jesus warned, building unity on anything other than the catholic apostolic truth of Scripture is relying on a foundation of sand, which the storms of history will wash away. The communion needs to restore the office of bishop to its apostolic roots in order to renew its true unity.

That's why we need Reformation Anglicanism today. We call on our bishops to prove themselves authentic successors to the apostles, not merely by the pedigree of their episcopal consecrators, but by what they teach and what they reject. We call on our bishops to be the chief missionaries spreading the Word afresh, when so, so many are strangers to the love of God made known in Jesus. We call on our bishops to be its chief apologists in this hostile age, defending the saving truths of Scripture from all assaults, whether inside the church or out. In short, Reformation Anglicanism calls on our bishops to promote and protect God's Word, that they may foster "truth, unity, and concord" in our time and pass these graces on to those who follow.

Reformation Anglicanism Is Liturgical

The Reformers realized that their plans for the conversion of England would succeed only if the English people regularly sat under the transforming power of Scripture. Consequently, Cranmer devised a systematic pattern of Bible reading for local parishes. Once again, he looked back to the ancient church for a model. Influenced by Saint Basil's example of encouraging workers to attend Bible expositions at daily morning and evening worship services, Cranmer adapted the seven daily offices of medieval monasticism into two services of Morning Prayer and Evening Prayer. A new lectionary which emphasized continuous reading through biblical books by chapter was also appointed. The Psalter was read through monthly. As the first lesson, the remainder of the Old Testament was read over ten months, "except for books and chapters, which be least edifying." For the other two months, readings came from the Apocrypha. As the second lesson, the New Testament was read three times a year, except for Revelation, which was used sparingly for certain proper feasts. As a result, most of the Bible was read through in a year. Cranmer's preface to the prayer book makes clear the purpose of the lectionary: "that the people (by daily hearing of Holy Scripture read in the Church) should continually profit more and more in the knowledge of God, and be the more inflamed with the love of his true religion." By fitting his Word-based services around the average person's work day, Cranmer was consciously trying to make Scripture-inspired stirrings of the heart an integral part of the normal rhythm of English daily life.

But Cranmer's commitment to promoting the power of the Word through the prayer book was by no means limited to the daily lectionary. It is a commonplace of Anglican liturgical studies that Cranmer's prayers stitched together countless borrowings from the whole treasury of the Bible. Indeed, what one scholar has said about the medieval English mystic Richard Rolle applies equally to Cranmer: "The full extent of his enormous debt to Scripture has escaped most readers simply because he was able to adapt the language of Scripture so perfectly and naturally to his own expression."[7]

Finally, for Cranmer, the sacraments were the ultimate example of the power of God's Word at work. Since human beings learn by their senses—by what they see, hear, smell, taste, and touch—Cranmer believed that when God's Word was joined to creaturely things like water, bread, and wine, the truth of his promises would more deeply impact people. That's why Cranmer believed that faithful communicants, not the bread and wine, are transformed into Christ's body. When the priest recites the biblical narrative of the Last Supper, the Spirit of God goes forth into the hearts of believers, strengthening their faith, stirring up more love, and uniting them more fully to Christ in mind, body, and will, that they might increasingly dwell in him, and he in them. Here is the heart of Cranmer's liturgical vision: divine gracious love, constantly communicated by the Holy Spirit in the regular repetition of Scripture's promises through Word and sacrament, inspires grateful human love,

---

7. John A. Alford, "Biblical *Imitatio* in the Writings of Richard Rolle," *English Literary History* 40 (1973): 1–23, at 8.

drawing believers toward God, their fellow human beings, and the lifelong pursuit of godliness.

Of course, in a time of mass illiteracy, Cranmer's liturgical plan for reading the Bible to the English people made perfect sense. But what about now? In an age when we have multiple means of accessing Scripture at any time does the twice-daily prayer tradition have any relevance? Perhaps it has even more relevance today, precisely because of the hectic pace of modern life. It has become ever harder to establish those boundaries needed to maintain regular times for Bible-shaped listening to God. Cranmer's goal remains the challenge for faithful Christians in every age—to find a way to immerse oneself systematically in Scripture, day after day, year after year. Adapting the principle of regular prayer to the natural rhythms of daily life is the only realistic way to success. Moreover, having a daily plan of how to read through the entire Bible is the only way to ensure that Christians sit under the whole counsel of Scripture and not just their favorite passages. The Reformation Anglican tradition of twice-daily prayer provides a helpful model for both issues.

But what about Cranmer's collects? In an era of ever-increasing individualism where so many churches have replaced structured services with praise choruses and spontaneous prayer, does the formality of using someone else's words to express the desires of our hearts not seem artificial, out of touch, and (let's be honest) boring? If the modern worship movement is any indication, it would seem not. After all, what is thirty-minutes of praise choruses but sung meditation, and the song lyrics but using someone else's words to express the longing of the participants' hearts? And whereas so many praise choruses focus on the needs and desires of the worshipers, Cranmer's prayers always express balanced biblical truths, not only about human longing for God but also about God's longing to love and serve humanity. Nothing better expresses Cranmer's gift at using worship to proclaim the gospel of grace and gratitude than his 1552 service of Holy Communion. In the final analysis, both Cranmer's prayers and modern contemporary worship derive their spiritual power from the same source—repeating the truths of Scripture, whether sung or said. Being biblically liturgical, Reformation Anglicanism has much to offer worship today, both in private and in public.

Reformation Anglicanism Is Transformative

For many people in the twenty-first century, Christianity has lost the spiritual power to transform peoples' lives and, thus, its credibility. One popular response has been for the church to nag people more insistently in hopes that if they try hard enough, they just might manage to change themselves. Another has been to go in the opposite direction and claim falsely that the gospel of grace means that people do not have to fight to overcome sin. Neither approach brings inner wholeness, because neither one draws people closer to Jesus so he can be at work in their lives. That's why we need Reformation Anglicanism.

Cranmer adopted the Protestant way of salvation because he understood that human beings can only be transformed from the inside out. The renewal of our affections is the key to human flourishing. As a Tudor humanist, he had been steeped in the importance of a Christian burning with love for God and neighbor. Yet, like today, many medieval people failed to experience that kind of passion for godliness. Consequently, Cranmer realized that merely knowing the moral imperative to love rightly did not empower a person to do so. Nor did the medieval church's means of nurturing it. Using fear, shame, guilt, and duty did not make love for God grow, and denying assurance of salvation in order to make people try harder only made it worse.

Coming under the influence of the Protestants in his forties, Cranmer came to see that the apostle Paul had taught a better way. Godly love could only come from personally encountering God's immeasurable love made known in his free gift of salvation. Once faith had captured the human heart and a person believed in Christ's saving promises, this newfound trust that one would be with God forever would set off a chain reaction deep within the individual. Justification by faith permits believers to experience the ongoing, indwelling presence of the Holy Spirit, who gradually transforms their deepest desires and longings. Under the Spirit's influence, the believers' trust in God's love for them leads them at last to truly love him in return. Now, despite ongoing sin and selfishness, believers have the power to love God more than sin. Here is the key to sanctification. For what the heart loves, the will chooses and the mind justifies. As the indwelling Spirit transforms their affections, believers give themselves wholeheartedly to repentance and godly living.

Thus, outward transformation begins with inner renewal brought about by the authentic apostolic gospel. Grace engenders gratitude. Gratitude births love. Love brings about repentance. Repentance produces good works. Good works contribute to a better society. Because of its emphasis on the Pauline doctrine of salvation, Reformation Anglicanism is the best answer for those searching for a means of authentic transformation from the inside out.

In Short, Reformation Anglicanism Is Relevant

For those in the twenty-first century searching for meaning and purpose in life, Reformation Anglicanism's commitment to the timeless wisdom of apostolic teaching provides a solid rock on which to stand. For those searching for a sense of historical continuity, Reformation Anglicanism affords a community with close ties to the ancient church as expressed in its faithfulness to Scripture, the creeds, and the first four councils. For those looking for assurance that God's love will not let them go, Reformation Anglicanism's proclamation of salvation by faith only through grace alone offers biblical hope.

For those who make the needs of others a top priority, Reformation Anglicanism's focus on mission encourages what God has already put on their hearts. For those looking for leadership in apologetics as the basis for Christian unity and outreach, Reformation Anglicanism consecrates bishops equipped for this specific purpose. For those looking to be sustained by inspiring, systematic, Scripture-shaped worship, Reformation Anglicanism's liturgical heritage offers the best model for proclaiming the gospel of grace and gratitude with ancient beauty and contemporary sensitivity. For those looking for real change in themselves and in society, Reformation Anglicanism's insight into the renewal of human affections provides the most authentic means to experience human flourishing.

We need Reformation Anglicanism in the twenty-first century because its principles uniquely address the contemporary needs and idols of our global society so that the glory of God may be revealed in our time.

Bibliography

Allen, Rosamond S., ed. *Richard Rolle: The English Writings*. New York: Paulist, 1988.

Allison, C. F. *The Rise of Moralism: The Proclamation of the Gospel from Hooker to Taylor*. New York: Seabury, 1966.

Avis, Paul. *Anglicanism and the Christian Church*. Edinburgh: T&T Clark, 1989.

Bede. *The Ecclesiastical History of the English People*. Oxford: Oxford University Press, 2008.

Bond, Ronald B. *Certain Sermons or Homilies (1547) and A Homily against Disobedience and Wilful Rebellion (1570): A Critical Edition*. Toronto: University of London Press, 1987.

Chadwick, Owen. *The Reformation*. London: Penguin, 1990.

Cox, John E., ed. *Miscellaneous Writings and Letters of Thomas Cranmer*. Cambridge: Parker Society, 1846.

———, ed. *Writings and Disputations of Thomas Cranmer on the Lord's Supper*. Cambridge: Parker Society, 1844.

Daniell, David. *William Tyndale: A Biography*. New Haven, CT: Yale University Press, 1994.

Foxe, John. *Acts and Monuments*. Edited by Josiah Pratt. 8 vols. London: Religious Tract Society, 1877.

Griffiths, John. *Two Books of Homilies*. Oxford: Oxford University Press, 1859.

Hardwick, Charles. *A History of the Articles of Religion*. Cambridge: Deighton Bell, 1859.

Hilton, Walter. *The Scale of Perfection.* Edited by John P. H. Clark and Rosemary Dorward. Mahwah, NJ: Paulist, 1991.

Hooker, Richard. *Of the Laws of Ecclesiastical Polity.* In *The Folger Library Edition of the Works of Richard Hooker.* Edited by Speed Hill. Cambridge, MA: Belknap, 1977.

Jones, Michael K., and Malcolm G. Underwood. *The King's Mother: Lady Margaret Beaufort, Countess of Richmond and Derby.* Cambridge: Cambridge University Press, 1992.

Ketley, Joseph, ed. *The Two Liturgies . . . in the Reign of King Edward the Sixth.* Cambridge: Parker Society, 1844.

Kirby, Torrance, ed. *A Companion to Richard Hooker.* Leiden: Brill, 2008.

Lloyd, Charles. *Formularies of Faith.* Oxford: Clarendon, 1825.

MacCulloch, Diarmaid. *Reformation: Europe's House Divided, 1490–1700.* London: Allen Lane, 2003.

———. *Thomas Cranmer: A Life.* New Haven, CT: Yale University Press, 1996.

Marshall, Peter. *Reformation England 1480–1642.* 2nd ed. London: Bloomsbury, 2012.

Mueller, Janel. *Katherine Parr: Complete Works and Correspondence.* Chicago: University of Chicago Press, 2011.

Nazir-Ali, Michael. *From Everywhere to Everywhere: A World View of Christian Mission.* London: Collins, 1990.

Neill, Stephen. *Anglicanism.* Harmondsworth, Middlesex: Penguin, 1958.

———. *A History of Christian Missions.* London: Penguin, 1990.

Null, Ashley. "The Marian Exiles in Switzerland." *Jahrbuch für Europäische Geschichte* 7 (2006): 1–22.

———. "Official Tudor Homilies." In *Oxford Handbook of the Early Modern Sermon,* edited by Peter McCullough, Hugh Adlington, and Emma Rhatigan, 348–65. Oxford: Oxford University Press, 2011.

———. *Thomas Cranmer's Doctrine of Repentance: Renewing the Power to Love.* Oxford: Oxford University Press, 2000.

Packer, J. I. "The Status of the Articles." In H. E. W. Turner et al. *The Articles of the Church of England.* London: Mowbray, 1964.

Parker, Matthew. *De Antiquitate Britannicae Ecclesiae.* Hanoviae: Wechel, 1605.

Pollard, Arthur, ed. *Hugh Latimer: The Sermons.* Manchester: Carcanet/Fyfield, 2002.

Rex, Richard. *Henry VIII and the English Reformation.* 2nd ed. Basingstoke: Palgrave Macmillan, 2006.

———. *The Lollards.* Basingstoke: Palgrave, 2002.

———. *The Theology of John Fisher.* Cambridge: Cambridge University Press, 1991.

Rummel, Erika. "The Theology of Erasmus." In *The Cambridge Companion to Reformation Theology,* edited by David Bagchi and David C. Steinmetz, 28–38. Cambridge: Cambridge University Press, 2004.

Seifrid, Mark A. *Christ, Our Righteousness: Paul's Theology of Justification.* Leicester: Apollos, 2000.

Wallace, Dewey D., Jr. *"Via Media? A Paradigm Shift." Anglican and Episcopal History* 72 (2003): 2–21.

Contributors

The Reverend Dr. Michael P. Jensen (DPhil) is Rector of St Mark's Darling Point in Sydney, Australia, and an Honorary Associate of the Sydney College of Divinity.

The Most Reverend Dr. Benjamin A. Kwashi (DMin., DD) is Bishop of the Anglican Diocese of Jos (Nigeria) and Archbishop of the Ecclesiastical Province of Jos (Church of Nigeria).

The Right Reverend Dr. Michael Nazir-Ali (DD), formerly Bishop of Rochester, England, is President of the Oxford Centre for Training, Research, Advocacy and Dialogue.

The Reverend Canon Dr. John Ashley Null (BD) is a German Research Council Fellow at Humboldt University of Berlin and Honorary Canon Theologian of the Anglican Diocese of Egypt.

The Reverend Dr. John W. Yates III (PhD) is Rector of Holy Trinity Anglican Church in Raleigh, North Carolina (USA).

General Index

Scripture Index